Unthinkable

**Raith Rovers' improbable
journey from the bottom to
the top of Scottish football**

Remember this !!

Unthinkable

Raith Rovers' improbable
journey from the bottom to
the top of Scottish football

Steven Lawther Foreword by Val McDermid

First published by Pitch Publishing, 2014

Pitch Publishing
A2 Yeoman Gate
Yeoman Way
Durrington
BN13 3QZ
www.pitchpublishing.co.uk

A CIP catalogue record is available for this book
from the British Library.

ISBN 978 1-90962-664-5

Typesetting and origination by Pitch Publishing
Printed in Great Britain

CONTENTS

DEDICATION

For Grace Jean Lawther
May a part of you always remain a
Rover

FOREWORD
by Val McDermid

TWENTY years ago, I was driving down the M62 from Hull to Manchester, listening to a football match on the radio. Not just any football match. I was listening to the Scottish League Cup Final between Raith Rovers and Celtic. My wee team, battling it out at Ibrox against the mighty green-and-white machine that was Celtic. We scored, they scored. They scored, we scored. I was screaming at the radio, heart swelling with pride, shrinking with fear. Extra time, no more goals.

Then the penalty shoot-out. The German author Peter Handke once wrote a novel called *The Goalkeeper's Fear of the Penalty Kick*. Never mind the goalkeeper. My nerves were shredded. Ten penalty kicks and still nothing between the sides. Then sudden death. And Paul McStay, the Celtic captain and talisman, missed his kick.

We had won.

I had to pull over on to the hard shoulder because I was blinded by my tears. I sat in the fading light of a November evening in the shadow of Saddleworth Moor, a grown woman crying like a bairn because my team had finally won a major trophy.

And that's what football has the power to do to us. It engages us, it ensnares us and then it enslaves us. We are drawn together in an ill-assorted tribe, united only by the love that not only dares to speak its name, it positively glories in declaring itself at the top of its voice. Often with added sweary words.

The ignorant often sneer at those of us who support teams like Raith Rovers. They mock the quality of our football. They scoff at the lack of prawn sandwiches and champagne. They snigger at our struggles to carve out a decent run of results.

More fool them. What they will never understand is the way a team like Raith Rovers brings people together and reminds us that our communities still have a beating heart.

I feel like I was born into a wider family than my biological one because my father and his father before him were passionate members of the Rovers tribe. Their spirits rose and fell on a Saturday in tandem with the club's results, and they never gave up hope that this season, or next season, or the one after would be the one that brought us glory.

They passed on that love to me. Wherever I am in the world on a Saturday, from Sydney to Helsinki, from Moscow to Minneapolis, I check the results. I have spoken to strangers in Rovers shirts from the Bahamas to Bournemouth, and within minutes, we've found friends in common and shared our hopes and fears for the coming games.

And nearer home, when times are tough, they're a kind of totem that we can pin our hopes to. It is no secret that Kirkcaldy has had to weather some serious economic storms in recent years. At times like that, people seek a source of optimism wherever they can. And in the spirit of 1994, Raith Rovers have rewarded us. They won the Second Division in 2008/09. They were runners-up in the First Division in 2010/11. And this year, as if to celebrate the 20th anniversary, they won the Ramsdens Cup, beating Rangers, the other half of the Old Firm.

Twenty years ago, Raith Rovers gave us something to dance in the streets about. They did it again this year. And because we're true fans, worshippers at the altar of hope over experience, we know it won't be 20 years before they justify our faith again.

Maybe next year? Right? Maybe on the 21st anniversary, we'll do it again. Right?

You bet.

ACKNOWLEDGEMENTS

T HEY say that you should never meet your heroes but in writing this book I had the privilege to meet many of the players I adored watching from the terraces at Stark's Park. I found every one of them to be extremely supportive and generous with their time.

I would like to express my sincere gratitude to Julian Broddle, Craig Brewster, Colin Cameron, Frank Connor, Stevie Crawford, Jason Dair, Gordon Dalziel, Ally Graham, Stephen McAnespie, John McStay, Jimmy Nicholl, Brian Potter, David Sinclair and Scott Thomson. It was truly a privilege.

I would also like to thank Alex Kilgour, Paul McStay, Graeme Scott and John Valente for providing their unique perspective on Raith Rovers. Paul McStay's contributions to this book remain his own copyright and cannot be reproduced without his consent.

This book would not have been possible without the help of a number of incredibly generous people:

- Val McDermid, for kindly agreeing to provide such a stunning foreword.
- Tony Fimister for his generosity in providing photographs to illustrate this book.
- Richard Gordon for his early advice and encouragement.
- Simon Pia for his reflections on an early draft.
- Mo Quigley for her excellent proofreading skills and tolerance of my poor grammar.
- John Greer for the invaluable access to his contact list and excellent fanzine interviews.

- Steve Wallace for the loan of his impressive collection of newspaper cuttings.
- Paul Burke, Julie Peacock, Neville Lawther and all on the Raith Supporters' Trust Board whose interest and enthusiasm for this book provided tremendous encouragement.
- My wife Elaine Lawther, who as well as acting as an excellent sounding board and informal editor has demonstrated considerable patience and tolerance with my slightly obsessive relationship with Raith Rovers over the last 25 years.

Finally, I would like to thank my parents, Neville and Jean Lawther, for their love and, just as importantly, when deciding to move our family out of Belfast in the early 1970s having the good sense to move within seven miles of Stark's Park.

Steven Lawther

After the first few interviews for this project I quickly realised that everyone views events from their own perspective and after 20 years incidents, people, conversations and timelines can often blend into one another. Where it has been possible I have made every attempt to check the accuracy of events but in many instances I have had to rely on the memories and recollections of the people who were there. The stories contained within this book are therefore recounted on an 'as told to me' basis and any errors, mistakes or inaccuracies are entirely unintentional.

1

THIS IS THE ONE
Ibrox Stadium, Glasgow,
27 November 1994

PAUL McSTAY left the centre circle and began the long, lonely walk towards the penalty spot. He had set off almost immediately after Jason Rowbotham's penalty kick had hit the back of the net and as he made his way forward he passed the relieved Raith Rovers player making the return journey. There was no acknowledgement between the two men as they walked within touching distance. McStay was deep in concentration, head down, contemplating the enormity of the moment he was about to endure.

The Celtic captain was idolised by supporters of the Parkhead club who had christened him 'The Maestro'. They loved the fact that his family was woven into the fabric of the Parkhead club with his great uncle Jimmy a former manager and his brothers Willie and Raymond having also played for the club. However it had been Paul who had truly shone in the green and white hoops with his wonderful touch, elegance in midfield and uncanny ability to produce an inch-perfect pass.

The Celtic supporters had quickly adopted him as one of their favourite sons as he helped the club win three Scottish titles, three Scottish Cups and a League Cup. When he turned down the lure of larger, more glamorous suitors to stay and become skipper, his place in the hearts of Celtic fans was cemented forever.

McStay had started the day in determined mood. Despite his glittering Celtic career, he had failed to lift any silverware since becoming captain. The club had experienced five long, barren, trophy-free years since 1989 as they struggled to compete with Rangers, their big-spending neighbours across the city. For a support used to perpetual success he knew that it had been difficult, almost impossible at times, to watch their bitter rivals triumph while they toiled.

This was to finally be the day that their disappointing run came to an end. Celtic had fought their way through to the League Cup Final and with Rangers having fallen in an earlier round, only Raith Rovers stood between them and their natural position as winners once again.

Few had accounted for the stubborn resilience of the First Division side. Rovers had proved more than adequate opponents, refusing to bow to the script that most Celtic supporters had written. They began the final with a swaggering confidence and had the audacity to score first.

Even when Celtic had fought back to equalise and then taken the lead with just six minutes remaining, Rovers found the impertinence to level when some of their most ardent supporters had given up hope.

They had more than matched Celtic in extra time and had scored all six of their penalties in the shoot-out to place intense pressure on the Glasgow side's captain. It was a pressure that McStay was acutely aware of as he progressed towards the penalty spot.

He knew that he had to score to keep his team in the final. If he missed the match was over.

As he made his way forward, each step seemed to attach an extra layer of tension to the moment. Around the stadium 45,000 fans were anxious for McStay to reach his destination and ready to urge him to score or miss with every last ounce of the energy they had left.

His Celtic team-mates waited in the centre circle, drained from 120 minutes of football and the weight of expectation. Beside them stood a Raith Rovers team equally drained but buoyed by the knowledge that they were just one mistake away from making history.

Across in the Celtic dugout, McStay's manager and friend Tommy Burns waited, arms folded, looking pale and scarcely able to watch. Opposite Burns in the other dugout stood Raith Rovers manager Jimmy Nicholl, proud of his players and declaring to his assistant Martin Harvey that they were now just one kick away from Europe.

Sitting in the main stand was Celtic reserve team coach Frank Connor, the former Raith manager who had laid the foundations of Rovers' team and helped shape the Celtic captain's early career. His loyalties lay divided. The same was true for ex-Rover John McStay, sitting among the Raith support and desperate for his former club to win but wishing that it was anyone but his cousin Paul taking the next penalty.

Directly in front of the Celtic player stood Raith goalkeeper Scott Thomson, frustrated at his failure to save the previous five penalties and determined to make amends.

As McStay reached the goalmouth Thomson threw the ball high into the air. The Celtic captain slowed his walk to gather the ball, letting it bounce in front of him before catching it. The stadium rippled with anticipation as they waited for him to take his penalty.

He reached down to place the ball and seemed to linger for a moment. Perhaps he was trying to make sure that it was in the perfect position. Perhaps he was trying to focus his mind and disregard the intense pressure he was under or perhaps he was just trying to delay the moment a little longer.

He paced backward nine short steps and as he started his run towards the ball he knew that he alone held responsibility for the next few seconds. Score and the immense pressure would shift to the next Raith penalty taker. Miss and the misery of the last five years would seem like a mere appetiser for the pain he would inflict on a battered and bruised Celtic support.

In the commentary position, Jock Brown searched for the words to adequately portray the drama that was unfolding before him.

'Unthinkable, surely for the skipper to miss,' he uttered and the crowd inside Ibrox Stadium held its collective breath.

As Thomson dived, those associated with Rovers knew that in less than a decade their club had made the improbable journey from the bottom of the Scottish Football League to the verge of their greatest triumph.

This is the story of that journey.

2

GETTING
NOWHERE FAST
Kirkcaldy, December 1985

GRAEME SCOTT sat in his office at the *Fife Free Press*. He had an end-of-year column to write about local club Raith Rovers but was finding it hard to muster any enthusiasm. The last few months watching Rovers had been grim. Actually, the last few seasons watching Rovers had been grim.

He was well aware that when he was handed the responsibility of being the main match reporter at Stark's Park it wasn't exactly a golden ticket to the glamorous end of the Scottish game. Raith Rovers were not the type of football club who had glory knocking on their door every season. To be honest, they were lucky if it came around to call every half-century.

Most of their 101-year existence had been spent plodding along in the middle tier of Scottish football and the record books showed that they had only three First Division titles to their name, the last of which had been almost 40 years ago.

There had of course been great teams and talented players at Stark's Park over the years. Rovers had nurtured Alex James and Jim Baxter, who would both play for Scotland and torment the English at Wembley. There was also their historic entry in the *Guinness Book of Records* as the British club who had scored the most league goals in a season – an incredible 142 on the way to winning promotion in 1937/38. It was an achievement that many younger Rovers fans used as a last line of defence when being taunted by their Rangers- and Celtic-supporting friends in the playground, but it wasn't really an adequate rebuttal to stories of Premier League titles and cup wins.

The harsh reality was that despite the odd title win, the infrequent promotion and rare appearance in a cup final, Raith Rovers had never won a national trophy. They were a club that tended to make up the numbers in the Scottish game, labelled by club historian John Lister as the 'great tantalisers', flirting with glory but never inviting it in. Yet even set against these relatively modest expectations, Rovers were seriously under-performing. Graeme Scott pondered the full misery of the last two seasons as he tried to force some words on to paper.

Scott had started covering Rovers in 1981 as they missed out on promotion to the Premier League under manager Gordon Wallace. A late-season collapse saw them overtaken by Hibernian and fuelled talk of the club intentionally throwing the league. It was a conspiracy theory that endured among the Kirkcaldy public for many years.

When Wallace left for Dundee United in 1983, his replacement Bobby Wilson seemed an imaginative appointment having enjoyed five years of success at Highland League side Keith. Wilson took up his post with Raith's centenary season of 1983/84 already under way and there was optimism that he could be the catalyst to reinvigorate the club.

In his programme notes for his first game against Morton on 24 September 1983, he spoke of the opportunity the Rovers job had presented him, 'It is indeed gratifying to be given a chance to succeed at the highest level of Scottish football and hopefully some of the success and luck which I enjoyed at Keith will follow me here.'

It didn't. Rovers struggled throughout the season, unable to escape the threat of relegation. Only a late upturn in form gave them hope going into the final day. They travelled to Meadowbank knowing that a win would secure their place in the First Division if Ayr failed to win against champions Dumbarton.

The sizeable Rovers support inside Meadowbank Stadium watched the Kirkcaldy side keep their side of the bargain, but a surprise 3-0 defeat of Dumbarton by Ayr meant that Rovers were relegated. It was an unfortunate end to the season but the closeness of the finish could not mask the inadequacy of the team and the entire club to the challenge of First Division football.

John Litster later reflected, 'A centenary season should be a highlight in the lifetime of a football club and should have inspired the players to greater efforts. Raith Rovers' centenary was certainly characteristic of the majority of the club's history – it brought only struggle, disappointment and, ultimately, failure.'

If Wilson's first season was poor then his second proved to be no better. Despite his claim that 'we won't be in this league for long', the club struggled to adapt to life in the Second Division and limped through 1984/85. A poor start left them quickly out of the promotion race and although they won nine of their last ten league games, they finished in a disappointing seventh place.

As an Aberdeen fan, Scott had reported on all this with a degree of stoicism. If he had been at Pittodrie following his own club he would have just witnessed Alex Ferguson's Dons side clinch consecutive Premier League titles. Instead he was at Stark's Park watching Raith Rovers.

When Scott had phoned Wilson in the run-up to the 85/86 season he had found him in confident mood. The excellent finish to the previous campaign and four pre-season wins, including the defeat of a strong Hearts team, had bolstered confidence. Wilson believed that everything was in place for this to be Raith Rovers' year.

'We've got the same nucleus of players who finished last season so strongly and the players I've held on to are becoming better footballers,' he said. 'Remembering the way we finished last season, people are expecting us to do well because the players have proved that they can do it. My target is obviously to win promotion. After the experience of last season, it is important that we get off to a good start.'

They didn't. Rovers lost to St Johnstone and Stranraer and after just two games sat second-bottom of the league with no points. Only the inferior goal difference of Meadowbank Thistle saved them from the lowest league position in Scottish football.

Results continued to disappoint as the season progressed and Rovers quickly found themselves off the pace of a promotion challenge. They had briefly threatened a revival in November by demolishing Stenhousemuir 9-2 at Stark's Park, the biggest win recorded in the Second Division since the leagues had been reconstructed 11 years earlier, but any momentum gleaned from such an emphatic win was obliterated the following Saturday when the team travelled to Edinburgh and lost six goals in the second half against Meadowbank. At the final whistle there was anger in the stands, with Rovers' fans coming close to blows as they argued among themselves.

Wilson approached the referee and told him, 'I hope you're as happy with your performance as I am with my fucking team.'

It was a comment that led to him being reported to the SFA, although he maintained the abusive language had been directed at his own team and not the referee. The final, fatal blow to the season occurred in early December when Rovers travelled the short distance to East End Park to be dumped out of the Scottish Cup by local rivals Dunfermline. The Raith supporters left East End in the rain after the 2-0 defeat knowing that, with all hope of promotion long since extinguished, the result ended their campaign.

The impact of the loss was immediate. Chairman John Urquhart announced that the manager's position was going part-time in a cost-cutting measure, making pointed reference to the cup defeat in his statement.

'It's very unfortunate that this happened but we lost around £34,000 last year,' he wrote. 'Without the possibility of a money-spinning cup tie to come we had to closely examine our expenditure. It is regrettable that we had to take this step, but making the manager's job part-time isn't going to affect the playing side of the club. Bobby will still be able to devote as much time to that.'

Scott reflected on a miserable season and thought about his end-of-year column. He could have written a regular, run-of-the-mill article full of platitudes about how it had been a difficult year and how the manager was working hard to turn things around but that wouldn't have reflected the truly awful nature of the situation.

He phoned Wilson and spoke at length about the state of the club and the challenges facing the Kirkcaldy side. Wilson didn't hold back and told Scott what he thought was wrong, who he thought was responsible and just how dire the situation actually was. After that, the column wrote itself.

'Time to re-think at Stark's Park,' wrote Scott as he leaned heavily on his conversation with the manager. 'As the year 1985 passes into the record books, Raith Rovers' fans are entitled to ask whether there is any reasonable prospect of an improvement in the immediate future. Disillusionment on the terracing has never been greater as Raith languish in the lower reaches of the Second Division and seldom in recent years has there been so little significance attached to a season at such an early stage. A season which began in such a mood of optimism has gone badly wrong and all talk of promotion has long since ceased.'

He continued, 'Apathy is all too evident within Stark's Park and there are some who question the ambition of those who run the club and whether they really want to get out of the Second Division.

At present, Raith Rovers are a club drifting aimlessly, and unless remedial action is taken quickly, they may well sink without trace.'

He finished the article with a stark warning for all at the club, 'The time has surely come for a rethink in attitude at Stark's Park – or Raith Rovers face a future in the backwater of Scottish football.'

It was forceful and heartfelt, vocalising the intense frustration felt by Wilson and most of the support. For a local reporter to write such a damning article about the club that helped fill his sport pages every week could have risked biting the very hand that fed him but its publication passed with little comment from Stark's Park, perhaps reflecting the accuracy of its assessment.

With hindsight, the publication of Scott's article marked the beginning of the end for Wilson's time in Kirkcaldy. Coach Dick Campbell resigned soon after claiming, 'The standard of players at the club is just not good enough,' and after a home defeat to Cowdenbeath on 11 January 1986, in front of just 600 fans, the Rovers board decided that enough was enough. Wilson had not won a match since the thrashing of Stenhousemuir back in November and the club was languishing fifth from bottom of the Second Division.

A few days later, after Rovers had beaten Newburgh Juniors in a midweek friendly match, Urquhart broke the news to Wilson that he was no longer the manager of Raith Rovers. The chairman prepared the formal statement to announce the sacking, 'We wish to intimate the termination of Bobby Wilson's employment as manager of Raith Rovers. Results have not been going our way, although we feel there is ability in the team. The post will be advertised, and we hope to make a new appointment as quickly as possible.'

Urquhart added that he regretted having to take the sacking decision and was sorry to see Bobby leave the club.

If the board had hoped that Wilson would go quietly they were mistaken. Wilson was bruised by his time at Raith Rovers and his comments left people in no doubt who he blamed for the state of the club.

'I feel strongly that I've not had a fair crack of the whip,' he said. 'I was totally disillusioned with the board of directors, and the players have also lost confidence in them. They are not channelling their efforts in the right direction, and the right hand does not know what the left is doing. My former club, Keith, was run a lot more professionally than Raith Rovers who are heading down a one way street.'

He concluded ruefully, 'I thought I was improving myself by coming to Stark's Park but accepting the manager's job was the biggest mistake of my life.'

For the senior players at the club the decline in standards had been difficult to watch. Defender Chris Candlish describes the shambolic way the club was being run. 'We didn't have enough players,' he says. 'Most of the guys I played with were all leaving and we weren't replacing them with quality [players]. There suddenly was no money in the place.

I had to bring my training gear home to get washed; there was no team bus either. I remember going to Greenock in a car, with Bobby driving. I was thinking, "What the hell's going on here?"'

Speaking to people who were around the club at the time, there is a degree of sympathy for Wilson.

'I don't think Bobby knew what he was letting himself in for,' says journalist Scott. 'His time coincided with ever decreasing circles. There were cutbacks on budgets on and off the pitch. He was a good guy but he wasn't given the tools to work with. He was scraping the barrel in terms of who he could recruit.'

Candlish agreed. 'It wasn't really Bobby's fault,' says the former Rovers player. 'The club had no money and was going nowhere. It really was hand to mouth from Saturday to Saturday.'

Former captain Donald Urquhart felt the manager was simply in the wrong place at the wrong time.

'Bobby tried hard but he wasn't the man to take the club forward,' he says. 'The whole club was so low from top to bottom. The club meant everything to me and it was so bad. Players were coming in who just didn't have it. It killed me because I loved Raith Rovers.'

Regardless of exactly who was to blame for the position Raith Rovers found themselves in, it was clear the Kirkcaldy club had reached one of the lowest points of its 101-year existence.

The situation was worsened by the fact that the local ice hockey team, Fife Flyers, had recently won the British Championship and were playing to increasingly large crowds.

Rovers were in danger of being abandoned by the Kirkcaldy public. As Scott started the calls to find out who was being considered as a replacement for Wilson, he was certain of one thing: given the dismal situation on and off the field at Stark's Park, the next manager would need to be something of a miracle worker.

3

OUR FRANK
Motherwell, February 1986

FRANK CONNOR was sitting at home when his telephone rang. It was John Urquhart phoning from the Stark's Park boardroom and he wanted to speak about the manager's position at Raith Rovers. It wasn't a call that Connor was expecting.

'It was out of the blue,' says Connor. 'I don't really know the full story of what happened but they must have seen it in the papers, "Connor sacked at Celtic".'

Connor is one of life's enthusiasts. He was born in Blantyre in 1936 and played the game from an early age. At only 5ft 8in he was considered by many to be too small to be a goalkeeper but he went on to sign for Celtic and made his first appearance in a 3-2 League Cup victory over Partick Thistle.

He made a total of eight appearances for the Glasgow club before moving to Northern Ireland to play for Portadown and Derry City. When he returned to Scotland to play for Albion Rovers he started to take on responsibility for coaching. His demanding methods resulted in some of the part-time players complaining to the chairman that they couldn't get up for work in the morning. Connor's response was typically robust. 'Fuck off, you're men,' he told them.

In 1974, Connor moved into management with Cowdenbeath, then Berwick Rangers, before becoming an assistant to Jock

Wallace at Motherwell. In 1983, he was finally offered a return to his former club, Celtic, as assistant manager to Davie Hay. He was delighted to be back in the east end of Glasgow, even if it had been a long and arduous route to get there. He admits there were times when he thought he would never return.

'There's always an easy path up the mountain but I just kept missing the sign,' he says. 'I once asked Jock Stein how I could get a better job in the game. He told me, "You first have to live in the jungle and learn your trade." I just said, "Live in it? I've been in there so long that I know the natives by their first names."'

His return to Celtic Park fulfilled a personal ambition to work again at the top of Scottish football. He loved the club and the intensity of the Old Firm rivalry with Rangers.

'A lot of people would have loved to have done what I got to do,' says Connor. 'I was at the Old Firm as a player and to be involved in the Old Firm again was great. You could cut out the atmosphere and put it in blocks. It was a magnificent thing.'

His undoubted passion for the role made his dismissal at the start of 1986 all the more shocking. As Celtic chased the Premier Division championship, manager Hay announced that Connor's services were no longer required. In a short, brutal statement he announced his intention to go it alone for the remainder of the season, 'After discussing the matter with the board and been given their full approval, I've decided to carry on working without the assistance of Frank Connor. This unpleasant step was taken by me after much deliberation, in the best interests of Celtic.'

It was a decision that devastated Connor. Press reports at the time talked of 'simmering differences' between manager and assistant, but to this day Connor remains tight-lipped about exactly what happened and I suspect that only those in his inner circle know how events unfolded.

The one thing Connor is willing to discuss is the hurt that the sacking caused him, which appears as raw today as it was when it happened. Connor's voice trembles a little as he recalls his removal from Celtic Park.

'I had worked so hard to be there and then it was taken away,' he says. 'No one will ever know what that did to me. It took me a long time to stabilise myself and I don't think the pain will ever go away.'

The aftermath of the sacking left him shattered and he describes it as one of the most difficult moments in his life. The fact that the newspapers reported that he had been 'sacked' added to his distress.

'It hurt because when someone is sacked it is usually because he is incompetent and I knew I wasn't,' he reflects on the decision now. 'One of my biggest problems is that I was too honest. I was brought up that way, as a man's man, but some people don't like honesty. I have been told that I was looked upon as being a bit uncouth, unintelligent; that I wasn't a Celtic type of person. That was hard to take. I fought with some of the players, but then it was part of my job to demand 100 per cent from them, and help them make the most of their ability.'

Most of those working in Scottish football had read the headlines about Connor's departure from Celtic Park, including Raith chairman John Urquhart, who was now on the other end of the telephone line. As Connor chatted to Urquhart, he realised that Raith Rovers might just offer him the chance for redemption he desperately sought. He agreed to travel to Kirkcaldy to meet with the directors.

The boardroom at Stark's Park was full as Connor entered. He sat down and began to outline his vision for Raith Rovers. He had a self-determination and self-belief that made him fearless.

'I always thought I was a top man,' he says. 'I don't usually say that to people but if you give me a couple of half-decent players who want it then I will do it for you or we will die. That was my belief. Never in my life have I ever been scared of anything.'

He left the directors in no doubt about his ambition. He says, 'I told them in my interview. I said, "I will tell you what I will do with you. I am going back to the Premier League. I am going back to the Premier League even if I have to take you on my back."'

His determination impressed the board and after further discussions he was offered the job. Connor persuaded the club to give him the manager's position full-time and he started to prepare for the challenge that lay ahead.

'The state I was in mentally,' says Connor, 'it was the best thing for me as I had to work. They were third bottom of the league but I thought, "Well maybe this is fate."'

When he arrived at the club for the first time he wasn't quite prepared for just how low Raith Rovers had sunk.

'When I went up to see the dressing rooms I realised I had dropped down a level,' he says. 'I am not knocking the place but it wasn't at its best. They had let the place go a wee bit. I sat and looked at the dressing room and thought, "Bloody hell! What have I done?"' If the dressing rooms were in a poor state the playing squad was no better.

'I took them for a couple of training sessions and I couldn't believe it,' he recalls. 'I couldn't understand why they had fallen so far. During Bobby Wilson's day they had allowed a lot of the senior players to go like big Tom Houston and Donald Urquhart. They took away the core and you were left with a few kid-on merchants from Edinburgh.

'I thought, "How am I going to sort this place?" I didn't know how I was going to do it. There was not a lot of money available for players at that level but I had to build the team again.'

On 2 March 1986, Connor took his seat in the Raith dugout for the first time, although he left caretaker manager Alex Kinninmouth to pick the team. In hurricane-like conditions Raith defeated Cowdenbeath 2-1 and Connor wasn't slow to make his presence felt, leaping out of the dugout early on to voice his disapproval at an offside decision. Just three days later he picked his first Rovers line-up for a game against East Stirling. They lost 4-1 and for the first time Connor had doubts about the decision he had made.

'We were getting beat two nothing at half-time against East Stirling and I am thinking, "Jesus, in the name of God",' he recalls.

Connor saw out the rest of the season and used the time to assess the resources at his disposal. If he hadn't realised just how hard it was going to be to persuade the Kirkcaldy public to love their football team again, then the attendance at the third-to-last home match of the season left him in no doubt. Just 254 people turned up to watch a Tuesday evening game against Stranraer. It was going to be a long road back.

His immediate task was to restore a sense of belief to Stark's Park, an attribute which remains at the centre of the Connor manifesto today.

'It is not just about talent and how good a player you are, it is about what you do with your attitude, what you believe in, whether you want to be a winner,' he says. 'At Celtic, even in the reserves, getting beat was a mortal sin. That was the attitude I was brought up with and I took that into Raith Rovers.'

Those who had experienced the club under Wilson saw an instant change. 'It changed totally the day he came,' recalls Chris Candlish. 'He had a natural enthusiasm about him that was infectious and it spread to everyone. He was no mug and he didn't stand for any mugs either. There was no nonsense with him and he sorted out a lot of people.'

Fife Free Press reporter Graeme Scott recalls his first meeting with the new manager. 'I went down and met Frank in his office the first day he was manager,' he says. 'The first thing that struck me about him was his enthusiasm and professionalism. Having been at a club like Celtic, Frank was professional to the bottom of his boots. Frank knew what he wanted and he wouldn't take no for an answer.'

Connor had a cause and that was to prove those who had sacked him at Celtic wrong. 'I was an angry man,' says Connor. 'That is what drove me that first year.'

One unfortunate supporter experienced the force of Connor's anger early on. He laughs as he recounts the story. 'There was a guy behind the dugout who kept shouting at me,' he says. 'I said to the others, "See if that guy shouts once more at me!" I turned around and the guy was about six feet. I jumped the wall and shouted, "Hey you! See just because you can't get talking in your house. See if you think you are coming every Saturday to shout at me, I am telling you big man, they will be selling tickets for me and you."'

When he returned to the dugout a policeman was waiting. 'He said to me, "Mr Connor you need to watch what you are doing." I said, "I will tell you one thing. I am prepared to get the jail for that reprobate up there." See when I think back on it, I can't believe it.

'I was a ranting and a raving lunatic but at that point I was a really angry man.'

Connor's anger motivated him to rebuild Raith Rovers. Over the summer he used his extensive contacts in the game to put together a team. As money was tight, many of his signings owed more to his powers of persuasion than financial reward.

'Other managers used to say to me, "How the hell do you get so many players Connor?"' he laughs. 'I said to them, "I'm the best story teller in the world." I never promised them this or that. If it was a pound, then that is what they got. If it was a thousand pounds, that is what they got. I just said, "I will do my very best for you" and I got guys to come.'

One such player was goalkeeper Hamish McAlpine. Connor recalls how he persuaded the former Dundee United custodian to sign.

'I remember hearing about Hamish getting released,' he says. 'Hamish was a good age but he was a good professional. I was in Motherwell but drove up to Dundee and spoke to him. I always remember he was in the middle of getting his house decorated. I blethered away to him and I got him to sign. He said to me afterwards, "I just came out to have a talk with you out of courtesy. I can't believe I have signed for Raith Rovers."'

It was typical Connor. He had great powers of persuasion and could verbally batter people into submission. McAlpine was joined by experienced professionals like Alex Brash and Andy Harrow, who were fuelled by the same desire as the manager: to prove to people that their best days were not behind them.

'I brought players to the club with something to prove,' says Connor. 'Players who people thought their best years in the game had gone. They had maybe been dropped by their clubs and had to come down a bit but they came to me and I lifted them right up. I was very fortunate to get good players like McAlpine, Brash and Harrow. They were all calibre guys and they taught our younger players about how to play the game and how to conduct themselves.'

Connor supplemented his experienced players with talented players brought in from the Fife junior leagues like Glen Kerr and Stevie Simpson. His Raith squad was beginning to take shape and the players were left in no doubt about the standards they were expected to meet.

'When I went there I thought I will take as much of Celtic's organisation into Stark's Park as I can,' he says. 'We made everything a wee bit more professional. There was a standard in the club players had to work to and if they didn't then they got told really quickly.'

One player who realised early on that there was a new way of working at Stark's Park was Jimmy Marshall. Marshall was a carpenter but was made redundant when Frances Colliery had closed. His new job selling insurance meant that he would often phone Bobby Wilson just before training to let him know that he couldn't make it.

The first time this happened under Connor, he was immediately dropped. 'No train – no place in the team,' said Connor. Marshall never missed training again.

Connor describes building a football club like putting together a complex jigsaw. 'Unless all the pieces are there, it will not fit together,' he says. He wanted a squad who were professional and ambitious, just like him.

'It is one thing voicing ambition,' he says. 'It's another thing altogether achieving it. Ambition does not just come from the brain, and from the mouth; it must come from the heart and stomach.'

There would be no room for kid-on merchants in Connor's team. Everyone had to be a team player and willing to work.

'There are enough sore heads in life so there was no point giving yourself another sore head by bringing a big guy who is an eejit, into the dressing room,' he says. 'I didn't care if they were a jack the lad or a bevy merchant, as long as every week they trained, played and didn't let the team down. You play for the team; you die for the team.'

Connor also invested time away from the training ground. If he could handle players then he was also adept at handling directors. He quickly established good working relationships with chairman John Urquhart and director Peter Campsie. He speaks fondly of both.

'John and Peter became great friends of mine,' he says. 'I was very lucky that the chairman John Urquhart was a football guy. He had played with Hearts and he played with Raith Rovers. He was maybe a quiet man but he knew football; he played in it; he suffered the pain; he had the elation of winning and he knew the pressures and he knew how difficult it could be for players. That was a great help.'

The developing friendship did not protect the directors from the full force of Connor's personality. 'I said to Peter Campsie at the start, "We will go through a lot of hard times and some difficult times and I will win some arguments and you will win some arguments." After three years he came back to me and said, "That is three years Frank. I've not won an argument yet!"'

As he prepared for his first full season, Rovers remained unbeaten in friendlies with impressive wins over Rangers and Dundee United. The club won the Fife Cup by defeating Burntisland Shipyard and East Fife in a two-day tournament at Stark's Park. The *Fife Free Press* sounded an optimistic note as it reflected on the cup win.

'In completing their pre-season programme with a 100% record, Raith have acquitted a purposeful look, and the confidence which they will take into the season proper is fully justified,' the newspaper wrote.

Connor believed that it would be a two-year job to lift Raith Rovers out of the Second Division so struck a more cautious tone, saying, 'If the players we now have at the club play to form, we should be in with a chance of promotion, but there are half a dozen teams who could be in contention. We will be trying everything that is humanely possible to get this club to the highest level in the shortest time but nobody should expect too much too soon.'

As the supporters' bus pulled out of Kirkcaldy on the way to Stranraer for the first league game of the season, the Rovers fans on board wondered just exactly what the new season would bring.

4
GOING UP
Stranraer, August 1986

S TEVIE SIMPSON was in the right place at the right time as the ball broke to him inside the penalty box. A huge Hamish McAlpine clearance had been knocked on by Andy Harrow to Keith Wright. Wright's drive at goal had been blocked with the ball squirming loose to Simpson. He quickly glanced at the Stranraer goalkeeper and struck the ball towards goal. His shot hit the keeper's body but it was too strong and ended up in the back of the net. The season was only 25 seconds old and Rovers were already 1-0 up.

Dunfermline-born Simpson was an unlikely star for Raith Rovers. Just six month earlier, 'Bingo', as he was affectionately known by fans, was playing in the Fife junior leagues with Oakley United and working in Rosyth Dockyard. He had spent a year at Dunfermline Athletic but lacked confidence and a series of inconsistent performances led to him returning to Oakley for a second spell. At the age of 24, Simpson thought that he had lost his chance at senior football and resigned himself to life in the juniors.

When Frank Connor scoured the junior leagues for talent in the summer of 1986, Simpson stood out and Raith offered him a second chance. He made his first appearance as a 57th-minute substitute in the friendly against Dundee United and was a starter against Burntisland Shipyard in the Fife Cup where he impressed with some darting runs and telling crosses.

The following day he played in the final against East Fife and was singled out by the *Fife Free Press* as showing some 'flashes of rare winger's genius'. He would quickly become a crowd-pleaser with the regularity he went around defenders and accurately delivered the ball into the box.

Connor recalls the raw talent of the winger. 'There wasn't a better winger in the bottom half of the Premier League than Stevie Simpson,' he says. 'I remember when we played Rangers in the Scottish Cup. He played against a Danish guy, Jan Bartram, and he roasted him!'

Connor had originally intended to ease Simpson into the first team gradually but his outstanding pre-season form fast-tracked him into the first 11 on the opening day of the season. It took just 25 seconds for Simpson to confirm that he merited his place.

In a tough and physical match, Rovers couldn't hold on for the win and Stranraer equalised with only eight minutes remaining. Connor was unhappy with the draw but at least it wasn't a defeat. However, a defeat was to follow four days later when Arbroath knocked Rovers out of the League Cup on a miserable night at Gayfield Park.

Defender Alex Brash would later admit that he went home that evening and told his wife that he might have made a mistake in signing for Raith Rovers. Connor let the players know in no uncertain terms that the performance at Arbroath was unacceptable and at his weekly meeting with the press he declared, 'Raith Rovers will be a more determined team as from now.'

His prediction was to prove correct as Raith went on an impressive run and after 15 league games remained the only unbeaten team in Britain.

A last-minute Keith Wright winner against Stranraer in mid-November sent Rovers to the top of the Second Division for the first time and newspapers declared that they were now the team to beat. Connor was less bombastic and would only say cautiously, 'It is a nice feeling but nobody is getting carried away.'

Just as media interest in Raith's unbeaten league record reached its height, the club finally lost in a thrilling game against

Meadowbank at Stark's Park. Rovers had taken the lead through a Colin Harris strike in 23 minutes. Harris, who had signed in mid-September, had been struggling to break into the first team at Hibernian and didn't need much convincing to return to his former club.

'I got a call to go and speak to Raith Rovers,' he says. 'I didn't have to be persuaded to go back. At the time Raith were in the Second Division but I didn't see it as a step back or anything. I didn't have any quibbles about money because all that interested me was getting a game. The deal was done in 20 minutes.'

Meadowbank quickly cancelled out Harris's goal in the second half and with just ten minutes left they led 3-1.

In a demonstration of the new attitude around Stark's Park the Kirkcaldy side redoubled their efforts in a bid to save their unbeaten run. Harris scored with a penalty on 81 minutes and a furious finish to the game ensued.

Rovers launched wave after wave of attack down the slope and when Jimmy Marshall slotted in a third goal the large home support erupted, but their joy quickly turned to despair when they spotted the linesman's flag raised for offside. Meadowbank held out and ended Rovers' unbeaten record. It had been a remarkable run of eight wins and seven draws, scoring 35 goals in the process.

Former captain Donald Urquhart watched on with some regret, having left the club a few months earlier. 'I should have stayed because six months after I left, Frank Connor was the manager,' he says. 'He gave the club a new lease of life. He was a great motivator.'

That Connor could motivate players was never in doubt and those who worked with him cite it as his greatest quality.

'His man management and his enthusiasm were excellent,' says John McStay, who had worked with Frank at Motherwell, and would later sign for Raith. 'Frank knew who he would have to put an arm around and he knew who he could give a cuff around the ear. He just knew how to get the best out of you. He is honest; what you see is what you get with Frank. If you work hard for him, he will do the same for you.'

Connor's approach would probably be characterised today as 'old school' but it was effective.

'I don't know if Frank's methods, the swearing at people and the shouting at people, would suit some of the spoiled players nowadays,' laughs McStay. 'I don't know whether you would get away with that. All these players with their fancy hairdos and their fancy boots, Frank wouldn't have stood for that, no chance!'

Connor admits that he doesn't suffer fools gladly. 'I hate dishonesty, I hate cheats, I hate anybody trying to kid on,' he says. 'When I took the boys on to the training ground, before we started we used to have a great laugh and joke, but when we started there was no kidding on. You have to do it right. That is the only way you are ever going to achieve anything.'

Connor's philosophy of honesty and hard work had been shaped by the great managers he had encountered in his football career. Jock Stein, Neil Mochan, Billy McNeill, Sean Fallon and Jock Wallace would all infuse him with ideas and self-belief and he brought that to Raith Rovers.

Privately, Connor had fears about failing at Raith and what that would mean for his career and chance to return to the top of the Scottish game. For other people such fear would make them cautious and hesitant, but for Connor it simply made him work harder and demand more of his team. He demanded the same level of commitment from his players as he demanded of himself. His wife would tease him about it.

'She used to say to me, "You can't ask everybody to be like you, you will drive them crazy," but I was that determined. It meant everything to me.' He adds, 'I used to say to the players go on and tell people who you are. You go and show them on the park. I knew all my players and they would have done anything for me. They would have given me the shirt off their back.'

As Raith Rovers continued to challenge near the top of the league in the first few months of 1987, Connor strengthened his backroom team by bringing in Murray Cheyne, a former colleague at Berwick.

'Murray has never been mentioned anywhere but he played a big, big part,' says Connor. 'He was in the dressing room. He knew all the players. He kept the mood of the dressing room right. We were a very good team. Murray knew me and we clicked from the very first day we worked together.'

Strengthening his playing squad was less straightforward as the club was still operating at a loss and in a weak financial position. Keith Wright was sold to Dundee for £40,000 but most of the income was swallowed up by the non-football side of the club. Wright left with a glowing endorsement of his manager and his team-mates.

'There is no doubt in my mind that Raith will win promotion this season,' he said. 'As far as I am concerned the other teams are fighting for second place.'

In February fate handed Connor an opportunity to add another experienced player to his squad. It was to prove one of the most significant signings in the history of Raith Rovers.

Gordon Dalziel was born in Motherwell in 1962 and from an early age showed great promise as a footballer. As a teenager he made the transition from Bonkle Youth club to Glasgow Rangers, a daunting prospect for a young player.

'I was just a young kid and you go in to the dressing room which was full of the experienced players that they had,' says Dalziel. 'It was hard but Davie Cooper took me under his wing.'

The young striker soon witnessed the quality in the first team, 'The first ever practice game I had with Rangers, I was told to go and mark Alex McDonald and it was the most frightening 90 minutes I have ever had in my life. Couldn't get near the guy! I was only a young boy and he was making all sorts of runs. One minute he would be next to me and the next minute, bang, he would be in the box scoring a goal.'

Dalziel adapted to life at Rangers and in 1979, aged just 17, he made his debut for the club as a substitute in a League Cup game against Clyde. He was to make his Old Firm bow in a match against Celtic in 1981.

Dalziel recalls the occasion, 'I was a young boy and growing up I always wanted to play in a Rangers game against Celtic. In my first Old Firm game I didn't even know I was playing. I thought I was just there to carry the hampers and just to pick up a wee bit of experience, but John Greig named me in the team. It was my first Old Firm game and I was nervous.

'I had never played in anything like that before and I remember saying to Coop, "What am I going to do here?" He told me just to make runs and he would find me. I was lucky enough to score after five or six minutes. The following week I was playing in the League Cup Final against Dundee United. It was a good couple of weeks.'

Dalziel's early promise never quite materialised into the illustrious Rangers career he had imagined and he left the club for Manchester City in 1983.

'If I am being honest, I probably had too much too young,' says the striker. 'I was earning too much money and I was living the life that I shouldn't have lived. Then you go from Rangers to Manchester City and get the houses, the cars, the trappings that go along with it. You tend to forget the most important thing, which was the football.'

He returned to Glasgow to join Partick Thistle and by the summer of 1986 was playing for East Stirling on a month-to-month contract.

'I was sitting in the dressing room waiting to go out in front of 80 people and one of my team-mates asked, "What the fuck is someone like you doing here?"' recalls Dalziel. 'That was when I realised I had let myself slide from the top club in the country to the one at the bottom.'

He was contemplating giving up on football for good, 'I didn't see any future in the game. I had lost the love of the game and I had lost the trust of people in the game.'

If Dalziel was destined to be another young Scottish talent who would drift anonymously out of the game then no one told Frank Connor.

Dalziel arrived at Stark's Park on 24 January 1987, with his East Stirling team-mates. He was visibly out of shape and substituted after 81 minutes, but not before catching the eye of the Rovers manager.

Connor remembers the moment, 'Gordon Dalziel came out a wee bit overweight. I said to Murray, "There is Gordon Dalziel. I am going to go see him and find out what is going on."'

The striker lived in Motherwell and it wasn't long before Frank had tracked him down. 'I got his address and went up and chapped his door,' says Connor.

Dalziel vividly recalls the moment, 'I opened the door at nine o'clock in the morning and there was this wee guy standing there, immaculate with a suit on, clean-shaven and his first words to me were, "You're an arsehole!"'

Dalziel was taken aback, but was aware of the Rovers manager and his reputation. 'I knew Frank and what kind of person he was,' says Dalziel. 'I'd never been in his company but I just knew he was a hard taskmaster and he was demanding of players. I knew guys like Charlie Nicholas at Celtic spoke very highly of Frank.'

He respected his directness and had no hesitation in inviting him into his house. Over a cup of tea, Connor outlined his plans for the striker.

'At first I said, "I'm not interested",' says Dalziel. 'But Frank said, "Give me a month, one month, that's all I ask of you. If I can't get you back to where you belong in one month then I'll shake your hand and you go your way and I'll go mine."'

Dalziel agreed to give Connor a month. The striker was out of shape and was, initially at least, a reluctant pupil. 'He took me down to Strathclyde Park and I had looked up at the heavens and knew it was going to start pouring,' says Dalziel. 'So I tried to pull a fast one and put a pair of training shoes on. I said, "Frank, I can't do this. It's pissing down and I've only got a pair of trainers on. I'll be falling all over the place."

'He looked down at me and said "What size are you?" I told him I was a size nine and he opened the boot of his car and he had pairs and pairs of boots. He threw me a nine and said, "Try them on."

'That was Frank. There was no hiding place and you never got the better of him.'

Connor skirts diplomatically around the striker's lack of motivation. 'Training wasn't his best attribute shall we say,' he recounts. 'He worked hard when he had to work but he wouldn't have volunteered. I took him for training. We started out like that and we became good friends, very good friends and he got fit and he played.'

Dalziel made his debut for Raith Rovers on 28 February 1987, scoring in a 2-2 draw with Stirling Albion.

In his post-match comments the manager praised his new striker, saying, 'Gordon is not yet as sharp as he can be, but we gave him his motivation again and his attitude is tremendous.'

His debut goal had much greater significance for Dalziel than simply earning his new club a point. It was an early indication that he made the right choice in coming to Raith Rovers.

'I don't remember a lot of stuff but I remember that goal because it signalled the start of that Raith Rovers era for me,' he says. 'I think if I had gone maybe two or three games without scoring, I might just have walked away. I probably would have thought it is too far to travel and more than likely walked away. It was an important goal in the sense that it pushed me on.'

The affection Connor has for the striker remains strong today. However, when asked to assess Dalziel's talent, there is obvious frustration borne out of the potential heights he could have reached.

'He was a great guy but he was the laziest brute ever,' says Connor. 'I told him that. I said, "You're a useless person Dalziel" but then he scored us 30 goals. If Gordon would really have had the bottle, he could have been a star at Rangers. He had everything. He drove me crazy by not working on the park, by not giving his best at times, but when you think back on it he did because he scored the goals.'

Dalziel has nothing but praise for the man he credits as resurrecting his career. 'Frank Connor to me is the greatest person I ever met in football,' he says. 'He wasn't really a manager to me. He is more like a father figure. To this day we still phone each other and the one guy I trust with my life is Frank Connor.

'I have had my ding-dongs with Frank. I remember once when he dropped me and I stood up in the dressing room and said, "I think you've missed something out here. Am I not playing?" He told me, "No, you're on the bench." I went into the office with him and it was total toe-to-toe but I walked out still respecting him and he never held grudges. He was just the kind of person I needed to rescue my career.'

Dalziel was rejuvenated as a player and team-mate Colin Harris recalls with fondness playing alongside the striker.

'Gordon was a great goalscorer,' says Harris. 'When he came to the club from East Stirling he was overweight. Frank put him through the mill but as his fitness came up and the weight dropped, he was unbelievable. He and I had a scream. We had a great partnership.'

With Dalziel in the side the club continued to push for promotion, although they were starting to develop a habit of drawing rather than winning games. When supporters booed the team after a disappointing draw with East Stirling, Connor vented his frustration at their impatience in his post-match comments.

'I was very angry at the attitude of the spectators at the end of the game,' he said. 'We are all sick at not getting the result we wanted but it was not through lack of effort, and the fans should appreciate just what the players are going through. All I can say is that we will be there at the end of the season, regardless of the doubters.'

The irritable tone was untypical of Connor and perhaps reflected the pressure he was under as the season neared its conclusion.

He attempted to relieve some of the pressure by adding, 'I would give my right arm for promotion, but it would not be the end of the world if we did not go up.'

An impressive run to the quarter-finals of the Scottish Cup, including an epic three-match struggle to overcome Highland League side Peterhead, underlined the ability of Connor's team but took its toll on the squad, who were rapidly accumulating injuries and suspensions.

Rovers reached the last game of the season with only an outside chance of promotion. A series of draws in the final few matches meant that they had slipped to two points behind Ayr United with the one fixture left. With only two points for a win, Rovers had to beat Stranraer on the last day and hope that Ayr lost. Thankfully Raith had the far superior goal difference so didn't need to worry about how much they won by.

The other factor in their favour was that Ayr had to play Stirling Albion who sat level with Rovers and had an outside chance of going up if Rovers failed to win. It was a complicated scenario and one which guaranteed a few twists and turns on the final day.

Connor was upbeat in public, 'We have to go out and win the game and just hope the other result goes with us. The breaks have gone against us all season, and we are due a bit of luck on our side. If ever a team deserved to be promoted, it is Raith Rovers.'

Privately he feared the worst. 'I couldn't believe it,' he says. 'The intense pressure we were under and Stranraer was one of the worst places to go to need to win. It was a tight wee park and they had nothing to play for.'

A modest travelling support set out from Kirkcaldy heading for Stranraer and the mood on the buses was one of hopeful optimism. Having staged an impromptu parade down Girvan High Street on the journey down, much to the bemusement of the town's shoppers, the fans arrived at Stair Park in good voice. They were quickly silenced when Stranraer took the lead after four minutes and had to endure a laboured first-half performance from their team which ended level after Dalziel scored an equaliser just after the half-hour mark. There was better news from Somerset Park as Stirling Albion led Ayr United 2-0.

On the sidelines, Connor wasn't happy. 'We were absolutely hopeless in the first half,' says Connor. 'You would have thought we had never kicked a ball. I said to Cheyne, "I am going to strangle someone when I get in this dressing room at half-time."'

There are conflicting reports on Connor's half-time team talk. Colin Harris remembers a relatively serene manager, 'At half-time he was surprisingly calm, just telling us to keep playing the way we were and things would click.'

Connor himself remembers a more colourful exchange. 'I told them straight,' says Connor. 'I said I'll fucking murder someone today. All I am asking is to fucking go and play for Raith Rovers. I said the fucking support has come down here today and you are fucking hopeless.'

Whatever approach Connor used it worked, as within six minutes of the restart Rovers had scored three times to lead 4-1. With a Raith win now virtually guaranteed, everyone's focus shifted to what was happening in the match at Ayr. The news was positive as Ayr missed a penalty then conceded a third goal, meaning they now had to score three times to deny Rovers promotion.

It was an unlikely scenario but when Ayr scored twice at Somerset Park the tension became unbearable. There were still 15 minutes to go and another Ayr goal meant that it would be them and not Rovers who were promoted to the First Division.

Graeme Scott, reporting on the game for the *Fife Free Press*, recalls the drama. 'I remember having my ear pressed to the radio listening for what was going on down at Ayr,' says Scott. 'Raith had won their game and that was game over. The tension was unbelievable as we listened to Ayr coming back at Stirling Albion.'

The Rovers backroom team had commandeered a radio from a supporter and were also listening to the commentary from Somerset Park but Connor was desperately trying to ignore it.

'I just tried to concentrate on our own game,' he says. 'There was someone behind the dugout with a radio. I said to Cheyne at one point, "Get him to get that bloody thing out of my road. I'm going to end up punching someone if Ayr score."'

Connor sat down with his head in his hands as the effort from a whole season threatened to unravel with a solitary goal.

On the Stair Park terracing the Rovers supporters were oblivious to the match being played in front of them and were desperately relying on second- or even third-hand information about who was winning in Ayr. The handful of home fans at the game watched on with a mixture of sympathy and amusement. One joked that Ayr had equalised, causing panic around the Rovers faithful before people realised it was a hoax.

As the *Fife Free Press* later described, 'The tension was almost unbearable as the minutes dragged by, and supporters not given to outward displays of emotion prayed for a signal of the final whistle at Ayr.'

There was no doubting the moment when it came. Connor exploded from the dugout to give a clenched fist salute as he heard that the Ayr game had finished 3-2 to Stirling Albion.

Gordon Dalziel recalls the moment. 'It was a bit nerve-wracking towards the end of the match,' he says. 'I heard that Stirling were winning 3-0, but Bryan Purdie told me that Ayr had pulled two goals back. However, when I saw the boss jump out of the dugout, I knew we had done it.'

The support on the far side of the ground reacted as they saw the dugout celebrating and some jumped the barrier to invade the pitch. The game at Stair Park was still in progress but the referee blew the whistle promptly to let the Rovers players and supporters start their celebrations. Fans streamed on to the pitch and surrounded the players. For striker Colin Harris it was one of the highlights of his career.

'It was a great feeling at the final whistle when we were mobbed by supporters,' says Harris. 'That was a real high point. I consider myself very lucky because you look at players who go through their career and win nothing.'

Later, as Scott tried to phone in a match report, Connor commandeered the telephone. 'I had been asked to phone in a report for a radio station and I was in the phone box next to Stair Park,' recalls Scott. 'Frank actually came along and virtually chucked me out of the phone booth because he had to use the phone himself.'

First claim on the nearest telephone was the least Connor deserved. It was an amazing way to end the season. He had achieved what he had set out to do but one year earlier than planned. He had reversed the decline of the club, effecting a remarkable transformation which culminated in gaining promotion in the most dramatic circumstances. He was naturally ecstatic.

'It was magnificent,' he says. 'My son came back from South Africa and he drove right down to Stranraer from Motherwell. I saw him after the game. It was emotional.'

Connor looks back on it now as one of the finest moments in his career. 'I have been involved with clubs who have enjoyed success, but that day was very special to me,' he reflects.

It was a special day for every Rovers fan who witnessed it, with the only regret being that they couldn't persuade the bus driver to take a quick diversion into Ayr town centre on the way home.

It had been a terrific season. The Kirkcaldy side were top scorers in the Second Division with 73 goals; the last team in Britain to lose their unbeaten record; and suffered just three league defeats, a record unequalled by any other team in British senior football.

Connor arrived home that night a contented man. 'I wore a lucky suit and a coat and a shirt and a tie every Saturday,' he says. 'There was a pair of shoes and the stitching had come away at the back but I said, "I am wearing those shoes until the end of the season." See when I went home that night, my wife threw it all in the bin.'

Speaking to the press a few days later he said, 'This is the first time I've finished a season and felt like I could start again on Monday.' When a journalist asked about his long-term ambition for the club, he immediately replied 'Raith in the Premier League? Why not! I'm not being flash when I say that. Dunfermline went from the Second Division to the Premier League in successive seasons. We could do it too.'

He continued, 'I found myself out in the cold at Celtic Park and I feel I've proved something by taking Raith to promotion and this has given me a lot of personal satisfaction. I've always said I'll get back into the Premier and now the gate is opening for that to happen.'

One way or another Frank Connor was confident that he was heading back to the Premier Division.

5

I KNOW IT'S OVER
Edinburgh, November 1990

WALLACE MERCER shook Frank Connor's hand and welcomed him to Heart of Midlothian. Connor had just joined the Tynecastle club as assistant manager to Joe Jordan. It was the return to the Premier Division he had longed for after being sacked by Celtic. The two men discussed the need to delay the announcement as Connor's Raith Rovers team were due to play Falkirk at Brockville that weekend. Mercer assured him that they would hold back the statement and Frank left Edinburgh.

He had not taken the decision to leave Raith Rovers lightly. Since winning promotion in such dramatic circumstances at Stranraer, in 1987, the club had consolidated and established themselves as a strong First Division team. They had finished fifth the previous season and sat only three points behind leaders Airdrie in third place.

His squad now boasted experienced players of the calibre of Cammy Fraser, Ronnie Coyle, John 'Jock' McStay, George McGeachie and Ian MacLeod. The re-introduction of a proper youth system under the guidance of youth coach David Hodge and chief scout Alastair McIlroy was starting to produce an excellent flow of talented young players into the starting 11, with Shaun Dennis, Ian Ferguson and David Sinclair beginning to make their mark. The experienced players recall watching the talented youngsters emerge.

'To have players like Shaun Dennis and Sinky [Davie Sinclair] coming through was tremendous,' says John McStay. 'Then later on you had Mickey Cameron, Jason Dair and Stevie Crawford. You would see them in training. They were good boys and keen to learn.'

The blend of youth and experience had helped turn Raith Rovers into one of the stronger teams in the division.

Raith, under Connor, had acquitted themselves well against Premier Division teams in the cups, drawing twice with Rangers in the Scottish Cup and defeating Hibernian in the League Cup.

The two ties against Rangers were particularly memorable. In February 1988, Graeme Souness had brought a Rangers team packed full of England internationals to Stark's Park in a match that captured the imagination of the Kirkcaldy public. The game was a sell-out and interest was so high that some unscrupulous Glaswegians were arrested for attempting to forge tickets. The police seized one batch of 800 fakes in Glasgow and believed many more had already found their way into the hands of supporters. The forgeries were of such high quality that it was hard to identify them on the dark February night when the game was eventually played.

A packed Stark's Park watched a tense match that ended up with the Glasgow side time-wasting for a goalless draw. Such was the lack of attacking intent from Rangers that some Rovers players actually sat down on the pitch in a bizarre conclusion to the match.

'We gave them as good as we got, including a header of mine that hit the crossbar near the end,' says striker Colin Harris. 'Rangers got scared and played out the final five minutes in a triangle on the edge of their box between Chris Woods, Terry Butcher and Graham Roberts.'

Rovers defender John McStay recalls a conversation with the Rangers player-manager during those last few minutes. 'Souness knew it was a banana skin for them the way the game was going that night,' he says. 'Three or four minutes to go and Rangers started to pass the ball at the back. Souness was saying to me and Ronnie Coyle, "Go on get the ball son. It's your home game. It's up to you to go and get the ball."

'We said to him, "You can keep the ball because we are on £500 for the draw!"'

The draw was secured, and in front of a crowd of 35,000 at Ibrox just two days later, Rovers lost 4-1. The final scoreline reflected unfairly on the Kirkcaldy club as they had taken the lead through David Lloyd and performed well until the later stages of the game when, according to Connor, the players' legs 'fell off'.

The following season, Rovers were handed another shot at the Ibrox club when they were drawn together at the same stage of the competition.

When Gordon Dalziel put Rovers ahead on 53 minutes at Stark's Park, the home support started to believe that a shock might just be possible. Sadly, their belief was to last for only 14 minutes as Rangers pounced on a slack pass from Ronnie Coyle to equalise.

Rovers held on for a 1-1 draw and secured yet another lucrative replay in Glasgow. For the second time in 12 months Rovers had frustrated the Ibrox club. At the replay, Connor was greeted by a visibly irritated Rangers chairman.

'Roy Waddell came up to me the second time we went to Ibrox and said, "Mr Connor, I am beginning to get fed up with you",' recalls Connor. 'He made it clear that there was no way we would be taken lightly. I walked into our dressing room and said, "I tell you one thing guys, we will not get out of here tonight without having taken a battering."'

The match was lost 3-0 but Rovers put in a battling performance against a full-time team packed with expensive international players.

Strong performances on the park were just one aspect of how Raith Rovers had progressed under Connor. Off the field, the club was now run as well as some in the Premier Division with a thriving commercial income. Commercial manager Alex Kilgour had been brought in and had rejuvenated the commercial activity. He introduced innovative ideas to generate income for the club like the Raith Super 10 draw, a new sponsors' lounge, pre-match entertainment at Stark's Park and the first free children's gate in Scottish football.

He was energetic and enthusiastic and sought inspiration from wherever he could find it. 'I joined the Football League

Executive Staff Association which was all the commercial managers down in England,' says Kilgour. 'We were the first in Scotland who asked to join. I used to get a round of applause when I turned up at meetings. The English clubs were miles ahead of Scottish clubs on commercial stuff and on community and it was a chap at Sunderland who gave me the idea of the Super 10 draw. It made us a lot of money.'

Kilgour heaps praise on the role Connor played in helping him with the commercial side, whether it was providing players for events, talking to sponsors after a game or being available to help charm and persuade potential investors.

'He was so professional and he was so good on the commercial side,' says Kilgour. 'He realised that if we got the money coming in it was going to help him with players. We wanted the Mercat Shopping Centre to sponsor Raith Rovers and I told him I was going to meet them at the Parkway Hotel for lunch.'

'Frank said, "I'll be there to help you" and he sat at the table with these guys and talked about his days with Jock Stein, Jock Wallace, all the stories and they loved that. Frank being there helped us get Raith Rovers thousands of pounds.'

Not all of the commercial manager's ideas met with the boss's approval. 'I thought it would be a great idea to have a real star come to Stark's Park to boost the crowds, the way Hibs had done with George Best,' laughs Kilgour. 'I said to Frank, "I will try and get some sponsors to get some money together to bring in a real big name." He said, "If that's the case, then you're going to have to get someone in to sponsor my fucking salary as well." It was a no-no.'

Raith Rovers was a club in good health, transformed from the club Connor had inherited. He was proud of his achievements but frustrated that they had been unable to make the next step up to the Premier Division. The impressive cup performances demonstrated to Connor that his team were very close to competing at a higher level but underlined that if Raith Rovers had ambitions to compete regularly at that level then they could only do so as a full-time club.

'When we played Rangers and Hibs I said to them, "All they do is train every day," he says. 'They don't have any more ambition than we have.'

It wasn't a new theme for Connor who had frequently lobbied the Rovers board to fund full-time football.

'If you weren't full-time then it was hard to get the players to come,' he says. 'You were only working two nights a week and trying to get to the same standards as full-time players was hard. I asked them to go full-time but they wouldn't even give me an extra night's training.'

It was to be one of the few arguments that Connor failed to win in his time at Raith Rovers and to this day remains one of his biggest regrets. 'See if I had got full-time, who knows what we could have done,' he says ruefully.

The reluctance of the Rovers board to fund full-time status had been a factor in helping him make the decision to leave for Hearts.

'I loved Raith Rovers,' says Connor. 'I really did, but then big Joe came to me and said, "That is you back in the Premier Division, starting to cross swords with the guys you want to cross swords with." I couldn't turn it down.'

Connor arrived late to Brockville on the Saturday and appeared distracted as he entered the dressing room. The news that he had agreed to be assistant manager of Hearts was being reported widely.

Ronnie Coyle recalls the confusion among the Rovers players. 'Frank didn't turn up until 20 past two and no one knew the team,' says Coyle. 'Cammy Fraser wasn't fit and he and I were just about to pick the team when Frank turned up. It was complete turmoil.'

The news of his departure rendered his team talk for the game redundant and the dressing room was silent as they prepared for the match.

'The atmosphere was terrible,' recalls John McStay. 'It was like there was a death in the family. It was like losing your father.'

The team took to the field in front of a near 4,000 crowd, including a sizeable away support that had travelled through to say farewell to their manager. The match was to prove calamitous as Rovers performed poorly and lost 7-1.

Defender David Sinclair recalls the game with a degree of horror. 'The defeat at Falkirk has to be one of the worst ever Rovers performances,' he says. 'It was one of those days when everything they hit ended in the back of the net. It was a nightmare from start to finish and the boys just wanted to get off the park as quickly as possible.'

At the final whistle only a handful of Rovers fans remained behind to chant Connor's name, the rest having left in anger at the result. It was an unsatisfactory way to say goodbye and a performance that still rankles with Connor. There was frustration at the way his departure had been announced prematurely and that his players didn't show the same fighting spirit in his last game as they had over his first five years.

'It never really worked out how I would have liked,' he says. 'It was halfway through a season and it was a hard way to finish. I told Mercer, "Don't let anybody know until after the game," but it comes out and everything goes flat and you end up getting beat 7-1 by Falkirk. That hurt me. You think why did you not do it a better way?'

John McStay recalls the manager's difficult decision to leave Kirkcaldy. 'He was pretty cut up about it but he couldn't knock it back,' says the defender. 'I do believe that if Raith had said to him that he could go full-time then Frank would have stayed.'

McStay was one of a number of Raith players who felt they owed everything to Connor. He had signed him in the summer of 1987 having known him from his schoolboy days at Motherwell. He needed little persuasion to rejoin his former mentor at Stark's Park.

'I wasn't getting in the first team as much as I would have liked at Motherwell,' says McStay. 'I was in and out so I took the chance and I took a free transfer. Frank was the manager at Raith Rovers and he came to ask if I would be interested in signing. You know what Frank is like. He wouldn't leave until I signed. I signed before I had even seen Stark's Park.'

It was a decision he would not regret. 'As soon as I went up and saw the size of the club I knew it was the right move for me. The place, the fans, it was like the place I was meant to be. I just loved it.'

In his first season he would win the Players' Player of the Year and Supporters' Player of the Year awards. As he talks now about his time at Raith Rovers his tremendous affection for the club is evident.

'I wasn't born a Raith Rovers fan but I am definitely a Raith Rovers fan now,' he says. 'They made me feel good up there and they made me feel wanted. They sang my name every week and I loved it.'

The former defender rates the atmosphere in the dressing room and around Stark's Park as the best he ever encountered in football. 'It was a great bunch of boys but it wasn't just the dressing room,' he says. 'We knew the fans as well. We spoke to them and had a drink with them in Kirkcaldy. My dad went to every single game I played up at Raith Rovers and after a while "Old Jock" was more known than me.

'You would go up to the 200 Club after the game and it wasn't a case of popping your head in and picking my dad up. You would sit and have a drink with the guys and if I had won man of the match I would give my dad the bottle and he would crack it open and share it with the fans. It was very special.'

Playing for Connor was also special for McStay. 'Frank would speak to me before the game,' he recalls. 'He would say, "People are asking me what I have done to you; what has happened to that Jock McStay? What have you done with him?" I don't know if it was all lies he was telling you but his motivational skills worked. It made you feel as if you would run through a brick wall going on to the park.'

Gordon Dalziel agrees with his former team-mate's assessment of Connor's motivational skills.

'Frank was never a great person for getting on the training ground and talking about tactics,' he says. 'He would do his job at two o'clock and at half-time. He would make you feel like you were playing a cup final every week. It didn't matter whether it was against Stranraer or Stenhousemuir. You walked out on that pitch and you knew that the manager thought you were special. That was a good feeling'.

'We had a dressing room full of egos but Frank had tamed them into a great team,' he says. 'And I think we grew as a football club, not as a football team, but as a football club. He was magnificent. Players would do anything for him. That is why Raith Rovers became the club they became.

'Raith Rovers were built on a foundation and the foundation was built by Frank Connor. A lot of guys like me and Ronnie

Coyle would never have gone to Raith Rovers in a million years. No disrespect to the club but we would never have crossed that bridge. Raith Rovers wasn't an attraction as a club, Frank Connor was the attraction. He started the rebuilding of Raith Rovers and he deserves a lot of credit for it.'

A major source of pride for Connor in his time in Kirkcaldy was the players he managed and, over time, grew to love.

'A lot of players I have met over my career, I will never forget them,' he says. 'Big Ronnie Coyle, John McStay, Gordon Dalziel. They were good people off the park and I would have done anything for them. All the boys that were there all had the time of their lives.'

Connor had inspired a remarkable turnaround in the club's fortunes and left behind a club transformed. The Rovers programme editor described him as 'quite simply, the most significant capture that the club has made in at least 30 years'.

Connor reflects back on his achievements at Raith Rovers with a strong sense of pride. 'I left proud that I had helped lift the club to a reasonable level,' he says. 'I used to say we need to put the concrete base in. It was no use digging up and not putting in anything solid. After the five years I was there, the base was there. If you look at it, a lot of those players played with the club for a few years as well so the base was sound and there was a platform for someone else to build on and maybe take them a wee bit further. They were great times.'

If Connor had rejuvenated Raith, Rovers had also rejuvenated Connor. 'I'll always be thankful to Raith because they gave me an opportunity and it really worked out for both me and the club,' he says. 'Raith took me on when I was at my lowest point and I will never forget that. I could have been out of the game if it wasn't for Raith Rovers. I loved it there.'

He concludes his assessment of his time in Kirkcaldy in typically understated fashion. 'It is only when you sit here years and years after,' he says. 'You just sit and think, "Aye, we did no bad."'

For five years Frank Connor had been the Kirkcaldy club's heartbeat. He had taken them from the depths of the Second Division to looking longingly at the Premier Division. Raith Rovers now needed to find the man who would help them make that next step.

6

HERE COMES YER MAN
Kirkcaldy, November 1991

JIMMY NICHOLL prepared himself as he got ready to address his Raith Rovers squad for the first time. Just a few days earlier, he had been at local rivals Dunfermline with no immediate thought of entering management. He recalls the moment he first heard of the interest from the Kirkcaldy club.

'I went into training on the Tuesday morning at Dunfermline and Ian Munro said to me, "I have had a phone call from Raith Rovers",' says Nicholl. 'He told me they wanted to see me for an interview and I don't know where that came from. I went to Raith Rovers and I was expecting to do the interview then phone Johnny Urquhart afterwards and get some advice on where I went wrong but I did my bit and then got called back in and Johnny Urquhart said, "Congratulations, we have decided to offer you the job at Raith Rovers."'

Nicholl was taken aback. 'When I got the job I was shocked,' he says. 'I phoned the wife and said, "You will never guess what, I just got that Raith Rovers job!" She said, "I thought you were at Dunfermline." I said, "I know that, but I am at Raith Rovers now," and that is the way it happened.'

The board had been impressed with Nicholl's enthusiasm and impressive football credentials.

Nicholl was born in Canada but had been raised on the Rathcoole council estate on the edge of Belfast. In his early years it had been a peaceful place before Northern Ireland was gripped by conflict in 1969.

'I loved growing up there,' he says. 'All we did was play football and go to school. Then that all changed when they started blowing up the city centre. People wanted out so they came to Rathcoole, then the Catholics had to get out and it became an all-Protestant estate. And then because it became an all-Protestant estate, they started blowing things up there and things started to get a bit rough.'

It was football that offered the young Nicholl an alternative when he was spotted by Manchester United scout Bob Bishop.

His first encounter with the man who had discovered the talent of George Best was fortuitous. 'I was playing for the Newtownabbey Boys' Brigade Junior Section,' says Nicholl. 'I got a phone call to say, "You're not playing for the juniors in the afternoon. You are playing for the seniors, as one of the senior boys is injured." So I went to play for the seniors up at the UC grounds in Belfast.'

A spectator at the match was Bishop, who was impressed by the young right-back. 'At half-time the Boys' Brigade captain, Raymond Miller, said, "Jimmy, there's a wee man who wants to talk to you." It was Bob Bishop and he asked, "Have you signed any forms for any clubs son?" I told him no and he then said, "Would you like to go on trial with Manchester United?" That was it. I was dead lucky because he just happened to be at that ground that day and I just happened to be playing. I shouldn't even have been there in the first place.'

Nicholl left for Manchester with six other young players from Northern Ireland. Their first night in England was to prove memorable for the wrong reason. 'There were six of us and we went into our digs about a mile from Old Trafford,' says Nicholl.

'Bob Bishop says, "Come on lads, I'm going to walk you all round Old Trafford." It was just to give us a feeling of the ground so we walked all around the ground. We never got inside, just walked around and looked at the size of the stadium.'

After the impromptu tour things took a sinister turn when Bishop took the young footballers for some chips.

'The rest of the boys were in the chip shop and I was outside with Bob,' recalls Nicholl. 'Then two lads came out of the pub opposite and walked past us. Bob said to them, "All right boys? Are you all right there?"

'He shouldn't have spoken as they heard the Northern Ireland accent. So these two lads walked straight back across to the pub which I thought was a bit odd and then came back out with a crowd of eight or nine of them.'

The young defender persuaded Bishop to walk off but the six young footballers were left to fend for themselves. 'They gave us a hiding,' says Nicholl.

When the battered and bruised group returned to their lodgings their landlady insisted on calling the police. As the person who had witnessed most of the incident, Nicholl was chosen to accompany the policeman to help identify the assailants, but by the time they returned to the pub the attackers had fled. It was a harsh introduction to life in Manchester.

The next day the process of becoming a Manchester United apprentice began in earnest and over the next few months the club assessed those who had been invited for training.

'It was a process of elimination,' says Nicholl. 'They just whittled them down all summer and you end up in the last few. You didn't really think about it at the time as you just get on and play but at the end of it I was chosen as one of the 12 new apprentices. It was brilliant.'

As he turned professional, and the conflict in Northern Ireland worsened, the club encouraged Nicholl to bring his family over to live in England.

'Football got my family out of Belfast,' he says. 'Manchester United gave them a club house, a three-bedroom detached house in a cul-de-sac in Sale.

'I said, "I can't afford this," but they said, "Just give us a fiver a month's rent until your father gets a job" and that is what we did. So I left my digs and went to live with my family, with my brothers and sisters.'

It was far removed from life in Belfast but his family settled and Jimmy eased himself into life at Manchester United. He would go on to become a regular in the Old Trafford side even if his first few games were demanding.

'My first seven games for United weren't great and I was sure I was going to be dropped,' he recalls. 'Then in the eighth game, I did something good, we scored from it, and the crowd chanted my name for the first time.

'On the Monday, Tommy Docherty said to me, "That's it, you're through it" but I said to him, "You should have dropped me five or six games ago."

'The whole point, he then explained, was not doing that. It was all about seeing whether I could handle it; seeing whether I would hide or not.'

Nicholl could clearly handle the pressure and would go on to play almost 200 times for the Manchester side, winning the FA Cup in 1977 when they defeated rivals Liverpool 2-1. It was an impressive win given Liverpool's dominance of English and European football at the time. He would also feature in the classic 1979 FA Cup Final when a Liam Brady-inspired Arsenal edged out United 3-2.

After spells with Sunderland and Canadian club Toronto Blizzard, Nicholl came to Scotland at the start of 1983, when he joined Rangers on loan.

It was to prove to be an eventful period playing for the Glasgow club.

'John Greig signed me on a Thursday night and resigned the following morning!' he says. 'A meeting was called. We just thought it was a discussion about the last game and the one coming up. John Greig goes, "Ach, I've been thinking about this for a while lads: I'm away. All the best!"'

Playing in a struggling Rangers team would prove difficult at first for the Northern Irishman. 'I remember a game we lost at Ibrox. John McClelland said to me, "Come on Jimmy, come with me. I'll show you how to get out of here." I said, "What, I've been here two or three weeks." He said, "No, no, you don't go through the front door, they're all waiting for us."

'He told me the players couldn't go through the front door because angry fans would gather there to give them a hard time. So he took me through corridors and tunnels and out the back. That's how bad things were.'

Things slowly improved under new manager Jock Wallace and Nicholl was a League Cup winner when he featured in the 1984 final at Hampden, a pulsating 3-2 defeat of bitter rivals Celtic after extra time.

After returning to Toronto and a spell at West Bromwich Albion, Nicholl was lured back to Ibrox as part of the Graeme Souness revolution. His second spell with Rangers was to prove more successful than his first as alongside England internationals Terry Butcher, Graham Roberts and Chris Woods, he helped the Ibrox side win two Scottish championships and two League Cups.

When offered the opportunity to assist with coaching at Ibrox, Nicholl jumped at the chance. 'I was at Rangers playing away and they bought Gary Stevens, who took my place at right-back,' he says. 'Walter and Graeme Souness said, "Would you like to start helping out on the coaching side of things and take the reserves?" I started doing that and it was my first wee opportunity to do the coaching side of things.'

As a football enthusiast, coaching was an aspect of the game that Nicholl had always had an interest in. Even as a first-team regular he would watch the youth teams train, paying particular attention to the youth coach's routines. The experience of coaching Rangers' reserves would prove a valuable lesson for his first entry into management at Stark's Park.

'When you are in the dressing room and you are talking in front of people like Davie Cooper, then you have to get used to talking in front of people the same age,' he says. 'They are annoyed they are not in the first team and you have to say, "Right boys, come on!" So when it came to the Raith Rovers job I had that bit of experience.'

The one downside of his coaching role at Rangers was that it limited his opportunity to play. When Jim Leishman offered him a starting place in his Dunfermline team in 1989, Nicholl jumped at the chance. He had played just over 20 games for the East End club when Raith Rovers approached him for their vacant managerial position. If his club career had impressed the Kirkcaldy board, then his international record was equally notable. Nicholl had played for Northern Ireland 73 times having earned his first cap in a match against Israel in Tel Aviv in 1976. He had been lucky enough to play in a Northern Ireland squad boasting the talents of Pat Jennings, Norman Whiteside, Martin O'Neill and Sammy McIlroy and under the mercurial management of Billy Bingham, the country qualified for the 1982 and 1986 World Cups. It was a remarkable achievement for a country of just one and a half million people.

One of the most memorable nights of his international career took place in Valencia at the 1982 World Cup when his Northern Ireland team produced one of their greatest performances to defeat hosts Spain in their final group game. Gerry Armstrong scored the only goal to secure their passage through to the second round, an achievement made all the more remarkable as they had to play with ten men for much of the game after Mal Donaghy had been unfairly dismissed.

Nicholl recalls the match with an enormous sense of pride. 'The game against Spain is one of the greatest games I've ever been involved in for a feeling of achievement,' he says. 'We were down to ten men, in Spain's own backyard, in Valencia, and still came through to beat them 1-0. The confidence we took from that was massive.'

It was an experience that helped shape his approach to football. 'If you're Northern Irish, you are always thinking of yourself as the underdogs. That breeds a refusal to take anything for granted,' he says.

'Whenever I needed to tell my players at Raith Rovers about what they could achieve in the game, it was always Northern Ireland stories I used to tell them. I never spoke about Manchester United or Glasgow Rangers, it was always Northern Ireland. "Here's what you can achieve when you put your mind to it."'

With Nicholl's impressive football CV, Frank Connor believes that the Ulsterman was the perfect replacement for him.

'Jimmy Nicholl played with Manchester United, played with Northern Ireland, played with the Rangers,' he says. 'So they were getting a guy who was involved at the top. To me that was where, looking back now, Raith Rovers were fortunate. With Jimmy and me they had two people who had lived at the top and had that drive. We weren't kidding anyone on.'

The loyalty that Connor had engendered ran deep and many of the senior players in the squad had been unsettled by his departure.

'We had lost Frank,' says striker Gordon Dalziel. 'He was our leader. He was what we believed in. When Frank left, I sat down and thought "I'm chucking it here as well. Nothing is going to be the same." Then there was this new guy walking in. He has never managed and has no experience. He walked into the dressing room that day and we were all sitting thinking, "Where is this going?"'

Nicholl knew that he was inexperienced and inheriting a team full of experienced, older professionals, fiercely loyal to his predecessor. He knew that his first task was to persuade his players that he was the right person for the job.

'I remember the first night,' says Nicholl. 'I said to them, "Listen, you are all Frank's lads and you love Frank and Frank did great things here. Some of you are older than me. It is a great opportunity, I think it is a great club and I want to help you to kick on and continue where Frank left off."

'I said, "If you are unhappy about something or if you need to phone Frank about something, then just do what you have to do."'

The players appreciated their new manager's openness and were pleased when he expressed his desire to build on, rather than dismantle, what existed at the club. It was a theme Nicholl returned to in his first programme notes for the Kirkcaldy club. He wrote, 'Frank Connor left the club in good shape near the top of the First Division, so I will not be making any sweeping changes. There has been an adverse reaction to Frank's departure, and it is important that we get a run going right away.'

Nicholl took time to adjust to the demands of part-time football, recording only one win in his first nine games.

'My first training session I was just straight in right away, saying, "Here is what we are doing"; says Nicholl. 'The pace was poor. I stopped it a couple of times and told them. It was only afterwards that Murray Cheyne said to me, "Jimmy, you forget that these lads have been up ladders and down holes all day. It takes a wee while for them to get going." It was an early lesson that Murray taught me and that helped.'

Nicholl initially left himself out of the team to give himself time to assess his squad but quickly realised that he could contribute on the park as well as off it.

'I left myself out of the team at first, just to have a look,' he recalls. 'I didn't want players up in the stand looking at me playing and thinking, "Who does he think he is?"

'I watched them and thought, "I can still do it. I won't be embarrassed if I am playing. I can still contribute." The boys used to call me "The Policeman". I used to stand in the middle of the park and say, "You stand there. Stop there. Hold the line there" and all that.'

The Rovers support quickly realised that they had not just gained a new manager but also a highly experienced and effective player.

'The one thing that it always came back to with Jimmy Nicholl was, he was a fantastic player,' says Gordon Dalziel. 'I hate to say that, but he really was a fantastic player. On the park you learnt from him. There were real good players at Raith but Jimmy Nicholl, for me, was a level above all of us and it showed on the park. That is where he gained his respect.'

Rovers finished the season in seventh place, well off the promotion places.

When Nicholl looked at the final league positions he realised that the teams who finished above Raith were all full-time. He quickly came to the same conclusion as his predecessor. If Rovers were to compete, they had to make the move to full-time football.

'We were sitting fourth and gradually towards the end of the season we were slipping down,' says Nicholl. 'At the end of that season I said to the chairman, "If you want to finish top of the part-time clubs every season then it's up to you but it is not what I want." Either we were content to stand still, or we made the move towards full-time football and had a real go at reaching the Premier League. It would have been easy for us to remain part-time and finish quite comfortably in the top six every year, but I wanted more than that.'

His chairman told him to go away and work out just exactly how much it would cost to fund full-time football in Kirkcaldy.

'I worked it all out and wrote it all down and I gave it to them at a board meeting a couple of weeks later,' says Nicholl. 'All the directors looked at it and then said to me, "Could you give us ten minutes?"

'So I had to walk out of the boardroom into my office. I came back in and Johnny Urquhart said to me, "Well Mr Manager, just to let you know, we are £30,000 in the black but we are going to let you do this for two years. Either you are going to be a success son, or you are going to financially ruin this club."

On 4 July 1991, full-time training resumed in Kirkcaldy for the first time since April 1970. The limited budget that Nicholl had been given meant that he couldn't offer every member of his squad full-time contracts.

'It wasn't totally full-time,' he recalls. 'We could only do it with the ones we could afford. I also applied for 12 YTS players but I only got six, but then two of the six were Stevie Crawford and Jason Dair.'

The move to full-time football would give young local players like Crawford, Dair, Shaun Dennis and David Sinclair the opportunity to concentrate on their game. Sinclair was in no doubt that it was a positive move.

'As a youngster you want to become a footballer and you want to be full-time and it was fantastic to go full-time with boys like Shaun, Stevie and Jason,' he says. 'Jimmy Nicholl used to make me ping the ball up the left-hand side of the park so I could use my left foot. It was wee things like that, corners, free kicks, the things you can't do when you're part-time. That made a big difference to us.'

Team-mate Colin Cameron, who would earn a full-time contract in the second wave of appointments, agrees.

'When you are full-time you are in there day in, day out, and everything is football related,' he says. 'I was two years as a motor mechanic and I did a year at sign fitting and I saw how hard it was. With part-time it is hard to throw everything into it. You are working nine until five and whatever it is you are doing, you are focused on that, then for a couple of hours, a few times a week you are then putting your attention towards football. It is difficult.'

Rovers started the 1991/92 season with the new manager still trying to find the perfect blend in the team. Some of his early selections frustrated the senior players who had been automatic choices under Connor.

'Some of the older lads weren't too happy that he was coming in to change things and change the team, so it was difficult,' recalls

Davie Sinclair. 'I was only a young boy learning the game, and as a youngster you just get on with it'.

One senior player who was struggling to adapt to the new regime was goalscorer Gordon Dalziel. 'Jimmy and I never hit it off at the beginning,' he recalls. 'We didn't see eye to eye because I was set in my ways.'

Reflecting back now, Dalziel accepts that at that stage in his career he wasn't the easiest player in the world to manage. 'I am sure I called Jimmy an arsehole and Jimmy called me an arsehole in the early days,' he says. 'But having gone on to management myself, when I look back on it now and think about everything Jimmy did, what he went through and how he handled it, it was Gordon Dalziel that was being the person who was the pain in the arse, not Jimmy Nicholl.'

He continues, 'We had been through a lot, had our arguments and all that, but we found respect for each other. Jimmy and I grew to have the kind of relationship Frank and I had, and all these years down the line, I would class Jimmy Nicholl as a very close friend.'

The emerging friendship didn't mean that Nicholl gave the striker an easy time. 'Jimmy called me into his office one Monday and sat me down,' says Dalziel. 'He says, "I watched you Saturday. You walk into the dressing room, you read the programme, you have a cup of tea, you walk out on to the park and you don't run and you don't kick a ball in the first half. You come in at half-time, have another cup of tea and then you go out and score three goals."

'I said, "Well does that not answer it all?" He replied, "No. See if you had warmed up the right way, you could have scored four!" I couldn't argue with that.'

The striker laughs as he recalls another incident at Somerset Park. 'Jimmy dropped me once when we were playing Ayr United,' says Dalziel. 'The team were going on the pitch shouting, "Let's get a result and keep Dalziel out of the team." I am obviously giving them banter back.

'I was sitting on the bench and we were drawing and I said to Jimmy, "See if you want a fucking win boss, put me on." I said, "If you want a win put me on, but if you want to draw then leave me sitting here." He looked at me and said, "OK, get on."'

Dalziel finishes the story with a mischievous grin, 'I scored two off the bench that day.'

The experienced striker began to form a prolific partnership with summer signing Craig Brewster.

'Every time we played Forfar, Brewster scored,' recalls Nicholl. 'If we won 3-1 he scored; if we won 4-2, he scored the two, so I thought, "I may as well have him with me than scoring against me." His football brain was great and he played up front. Brewster and Dalziel were a brilliant combination.'

Dalziel recalls the instant understanding he developed with his strike partner. 'Brewster and I just clicked,' he says. 'He was a talented, talented boy and I'll always remember a goal we scored down at Morton. I turned on the halfway line and big Brewster had picked the ball up and he just knew where I'd be without looking to pick me out. It was something that folk must have looked at and thought that we must have worked at in training but we never did. We just had an understanding. You couldn't coach it, it was just there.'

Brewster feels the same. 'I was a midfield player when I joined,' says Brewster. 'It was Jimmy Nic that put me centre-forward and I never really looked back after that. I always wanted to score goals from midfield so to be given that chance up front was brilliant and the partnership I had with Gordon Dalziel was phenomenal right from the start.

'Jimmy Nic changed my outlook on football by the way he went about things as player-manager of Raith Rovers. His enthusiasm to play the game just rubbed off on everybody.'

Nicholl added another gifted player to his squad with the acquisition of Peter Hetherston from Falkirk in October 1991. 'Silky' had no hesitation in joining the Kirkcaldy club.

'Jim Jefferies had told me that Falkirk was going to offer me a contract but no signing-on fee and I told him I wasn't interested, so I was put on the transfer list,' says Hetherston. 'Out of the blue I got a call from Jimmy Nicholl. I was going through a hectic time of it as my wife was expecting our first child. I met Jimmy at the Forth Bridge Hotel and then watched Raith play Clydebank that evening.'

The enthusiastic personality of the manager won Hetherston over immediately, 'Jimmy was absolutely brilliant. The first time I met him, I liked him right away.'

Hetherston fitted in instantly and quickly became an influential figure around Stark's Park. Defender John McStay describes the midfielder as the 'final piece in the jigsaw'.

Off the field, Murray Cheyne left to be replaced by Martin Harvey. Harvey was well known to Nicholl, having been Billy Bingham's assistant at Northern Ireland. Harvey recalls the initial approach. 'To be honest I didn't even know where Rovers were!' he says. 'I said to my wife, "I'm going up to Raith Rovers. Get the map out." So we got the map out and started looking. I found Kilmarnock, Montrose, Forfar, Dundee, Aberdeen but no Raith.'

Eventually he phoned Nicholl and realised that he should head to Kirkcaldy. 'I travelled up; spent the week with him. He said, "What do you think?" and I said, "Great Jimmy. Your ideas are similar to my own. I like the way you handle yourself and the players."

'Jimmy was so enthusiastic. He was so wrapped up in the club and the game it wasn't true, and some of that rubbed off on me and got me going again.'

Harvey would become an integral part of the Rovers backroom staff, having a major influence on players and on the manager's thinking. Nicholl is effusive in his praise for the ability of his former assistant.

'I got Martin Harvey and that was massive,' he says. 'I had worked with him at Northern Ireland, with Billy Bingham, and I knew what he was like communicating with players. He was a great help. He would also see things differently to me because I was playing. Martin Harvey was brilliant for me.'

Over the course of the season the squad developed a settled shape with a blend of youth and experience. The experience of the senior players helped develop the younger players and their enthusiasm for the game benefited the senior men. Rovers went on a good run of form at the end of the season and finished fifth, only four points away from promotion.

A highlight of the season had been a 4-1 demolition of Premier Division Motherwell at Stark's Park in the League Cup. The goal of the match was an audacious lob from winger Martin Nelson, which left Motherwell goalkeeper Sieb Dykstra deflated on the ground. The absence of video evidence renders it impossible to determine just how far out Nelson actually was when he scored, as every recollection of the goal by Rovers supporters added a yard.

Craig Brewster recalls the lift the result gave the team.

'The night against Motherwell in the League Cup was one of those nights the small teams have against bigger teams every now and again,' he says. 'It was 4-1, going on six or seven. That gave everyone confidence that we could compete.'

Nicholl was growing in confidence as a manager and the squad was strong, with talented players in most positions. Nicholl knew that winning promotion wouldn't be easy but as he examined the fixture list for the 1992/93 season he pondered what it would take to win the First Division title: confidence, self-belief, a slice of good luck and, above all, a positive start in their opening fixture against St Mirren.

7

SUCH GREAT HEIGHTS
Paisley, August 1992

JULIAN BRODDLE boarded the St Mirren team bus as it prepared to depart for Kirkcaldy for the opening game of the season. The Paisley side were newly relegated but hopes were high that they could make a quick return to the top division. As he looked around his team-mates, Broddle saw talented players like Barry Lavety and Paul Lambert and understood why bookmakers had made them favourites for the title. The first game wouldn't be easy, as Raith Rovers were a strong side but he was hopeful that they could start the season with a win.

The journey that led Broddle to Scotland can best be described as long and winding. It began in his home town when he signed for the club he had supported as a boy, Sheffield United.

Broddle recalls those early days. 'I left school on a Friday and joined Sheffield United on the Monday,' he says. 'Sheffield was my home town and United were the team I always wanted to play for.'

He fulfilled an ambition when, aged just 17, he made his debut for the Blades in the 1981/82 season, becoming the youngest player to play for the club. He found the experience daunting. 'It was wonderful to make my debut but I wasn't ready for it,' he says. 'I was too nervous; lots of my family and mates were there and I didn't really do it justice.'

It was to be his only appearance for the Blades. He stayed with United until 1983 but, frustrated by the lack of first-team opportunities, he moved to Scunthorpe. He admits now that he should have perhaps stuck it out and fought his way into the first team at Bramall Lane but he quickly established himself at Scunthorpe and over the next four years made 135 appearances, scoring 32 goals. In one of those unusual twists that football often throws up, Broddle's first goal for Scunthorpe came in a match against the club he supported.

'I came back to play against Sheffield United with Scunthorpe on my birthday in a night match and I scored my very first league goal,' he says. 'It was like a fairytale but it was strange because I was playing against a team I loved and supported and there I was scoring against them.'

His performances at Scunthorpe earned him a move to Barnsley in 1987 and he had three successful years with the Yorkshire club before his time there ended in farcical circumstances.

'I went to the changing rooms and someone was stood in my spot and had my kit on,' recalls Broddle. 'I said, "What is going on?" and they said, "You better talk to the gaffer." I went to see the manager and he said, "Oh, I have sold you to Plymouth Argyle."

'I said, "You what?" He said, "Yeah, and we have made a few grand profit as well." I said, "I'm not going" and he told me, "You have to. We've sold you and we can't afford not to!"'

It was an era when power rested with clubs, not players, and Broddle was left with no option but to make the move to Plymouth. He had barely had a chance to settle when the manager who had brought him to the club, Ken Brown, was replaced with David Kemp from Wimbledon. Kemp brought with him the long-ball tactics that had worked so well for the south London club and Broddle realised early on that life in Plymouth was not going to turn out the way he had hoped.

'The first training session was, "Right, the keeper will give the ball to you and you are going to launch it as far as you can. I don't want you to be playing it on or knocking it to the side." I just thought, "What?"'

The defender played only nine times for Plymouth and quickly found himself looking for his fifth club.

He reflects back on his early career and feels that a combination of bad luck and lack of confidence held him back. 'I'd almost get to the big clubs,' he says. 'I always got close but I never got that big one. I'd play great for one game, average for four, brilliant for two, shit for five. I was always up and down. It was just a mental thing.'

His next move would take him to Scotland. 'My agent said, "St Mirren want you, so let's fly up there and let's go speak to them."'

They flew up to Glasgow and the welcome on their arrival wasn't exactly friendly. 'When we got up there we got into the taxi and the driver was a real old, gruff Glaswegian guy,' he says. 'It turns out he was a Rangers fanatic so when we said, "Can you take us to St Mirren?" he said, "Don't talk to me about those Catholic so and so's." I thought, "Welcome to Scotland."'

His bad luck with managers continued as Tony Fitzpatrick was replaced by Davie Hay, who was then replaced by Jimmy Bone. Bone wasn't exactly Broddle's biggest fan but he drafted him into the team for the game against Raith Rovers at Stark's Park as the injury-hit Paisley side were struggling for players.

'I wasn't meant to be playing,' he says. 'I had a slight injury but they were short and he asked for people to play so I played, and what a mistake that was.' Broddle and his St Mirren team-mates took to the field for a match they would not forget in a hurry.

Gordon Dalziel recalls his team's confidence ahead of the match. 'We watched St Mirren coming in,' he says. 'They had just been relegated and you are looking about the dressing room and you are all thinking, "You know something, we are going to give you a game." We knew we were a top side. We just had something. We knew if we play we will beat anybody.'

The striker's confidence was not misplaced. He opened the scoring after just 15 minutes, and two minutes later debutant Jason Dair scored a second with a delightful chip over Campbell Money from 25 yards. It was a special moment for the young Fifer making an unexpected first league start.

'The St Mirren game was my debut game and I definitely wasn't expecting it,' says Dair. 'As usual, we were helping out at the ground and as the team was getting announced I was away to the shops with the lady from the canteen as we had run out of rolls. When I came back, I was quickly ushered into the dressing room and told to get changed as I was starting. It probably helped looking back as I never had time to get nervous or worried.'

Dair had progressed through the YTS ranks at Stark's Park into the first team. 'It was exciting to be going into full-time football,' says Dair. 'The other five lads – Andy Buchanan, Mikey Davis, Stevie Crawford, George Johnston and Grant Gay – were all good guys and we had a great time. Everything was new for all of us and Martin Harvey and Jimmy Nicholl and the rest of the senior players kept us grounded and made sure we never got above our station.'

Dair was from a strong football family and his younger brother Lee would also play for the Kirkcaldy club in later years. The press often focused on his family connection to Scotland legend Jim Baxter but it was his immediate family who helped shape his football career.

'My earliest memory of football was going to watch my dad,' he recalls. 'He played junior football and won the Junior Cup with Glenrothes and it was great going to watch him and getting to play in the goals at half-time! My dad has always been my biggest influence and I'm still going to him for advice today.

'The Jim Baxter thing never really had much impact. He was my mum's blood brother but was adopted at an early age and wasn't part of our immediate family. I only really found out the whole story as a teenager. We went though to his pub a few times and I met him at a couple of functions when I first broke through into the Raith first team.'

His debut goal against St Mirren marked his arrival in style and when Ronnie Coyle added a third with a flowing run and shot after 35 minutes, Raith were comfortably controlling the match. The second half saw Dalziel complete his hat-trick and Craig Brewster add a double to secure an improbable 7-0 win for Rovers.

Davie Sinclair recalls the match with a smile. 'We got an early goal and everything we did came off for us,' he says. 'It just seemed to work. St Mirren were one of the favourites for promotion and to destroy them the way we did, gave us a great start to the season.'

For the unfortunate Broddle it was one of his biggest defeats in football. 'It was a horrible experience,' he says. 'I have never been involved in a game like it.'

There would be a silver lining for Broddle as Jimmy Nicholl signed him for Rovers the following July. 'Martin Harvey and Jimmy Nicholl were there and, considering how shit we were, they must have seen something in me that day,' he laughs.

The emphatic win sounded out a warning to the other clubs in the First Division that Raith Rovers meant business. 'I think we went from 33-1 to about 10-1 on the back of that result,' says Nicholl.

The result gave the Rovers squad a belief that they would carry through the rest of the season. They knew that they weren't going to win by seven goals every week but they knew they had the talent and ability to beat any team in the division. Rovers followed up their demolition of St Mirren with two draws and seven straight wins, leaving them two points clear at the top of the table at the end of the first quarter.

There was no doubting the quality throughout Nicholl's squad. Gordon Arthur and Tom Carson were solid and reliable goalkeepers. In defence, Nicholl had the option of calm experience in Ian MacLeod, John McStay, George McGeachie and Ronnie Coyle, or aggressive youth in Shaun Dennis and Davie Sinclair. Ian Thomson, Peter Hetherston and Nicholl offered passing ability and composure in midfield while in attack, Dalziel and Brewster were bursting with goals.

It was not just the first team that was brimming with talent. The young players in the reserves were equally as gifted. Centre-half Robbie Raeside was an able stand-in for Dennis and in Jason Dair, Stevie Crawford and Colin Cameron, Rovers had three of the most promising players in the division.

Crawford was the next young player to progress into the first team, having taken encouragement from Jason Dair's scoring debut on the opening day of the season.

'Jason and I had played boys' club together,' recalls Crawford. 'I was out on loan to Rosyth Juniors at the start of the season and I remember jumping in the car after my game knowing that my mate had made his debut. I remember turning on the radio and hearing 7-0 and I was thinking, "Please just let me hear that he scored!"

'I can remember that feeling as if it was yesterday, when they said "Jason Dair scored" and I thought, "Jesus that is my best mate and if he can do it, I can do it. I want to be part of that."'

Crawford got his chance in November, matching his friend's achievement by scoring the winner on his debut in a tight match against promotion rivals Dunfermline.

After the match a nervous Crawford told a Scottish Television reporter, 'I used to be with Dunfermline when I was younger and it was good to score against them on my debut.'

The striker recalls his early career with the Pars, 'I signed an S-form with Dunfermline when I was 15 and in my fifth year of high school. I trained with Dunfermline for two weeks in the school holidays and Ian Munro, who was the manager then, said after the two weeks they had liked what they had seen, but physically they didn't think I was going to be able to adapt to professional football. They were right for the size and physical stature I was at that time. I was well short of it.'

It would turn out to be a temporary setback as Crawford was quickly spotted by Nicholl and offered a YTS contract with Raith Rovers.

'I went back to my boys' club and Jason Dair and George Johnson who had signed two-year YTS places for the Rovers were also playing at the same club,' he says. 'Jimmy was driving home one night and he came to a game in Glenrothes to watch Jason and George to see how they were getting on and I caught his eye.'

Crawford reflects back on his debut goal and the experience of breaking into the first team. 'I was delighted to score because Jason had done it and I had emulated him,' he says. 'I think the goal itself got a lot of attention because I had been with Dunfermline but they made a decision that was fair at the time and I didn't have anything against Ian Munro. He actually came up to me later on and shook my hand and said to me, "It is nice to be proved wrong."'

The chance to play alongside a partnership as breathtaking as Dalziel and Brewster was an apprenticeship that most young players can only dream of.

'Dalziel was clever,' says Crawford. 'His movement and finishing was exceptional. And Brewster, when you made your run, he found you. I thought the partnership they had was formidable and to break into the team alongside them was fantastic. I was learning all the time. We were lucky because we had great players around about us. The senior pros would tell you what you were doing wrong and what you were doing right. Sometimes it was a harsh environment but it brought us on and matured us quicker.'

Rovers stayed unbeaten until the first day of December when, after getting stuck in M8 traffic on the way to Kilbowie, they arrived late and lost 3-0 to Clydebank. The result did not unduly trouble Nicholl as Rovers remained clear at the top of the league. Indeed, he felt the defeat actually relieved some of the pressure on the squad.

Supporters of the Kirkcaldy club were starting to believe that their team might just sustain their challenge all the way through to the end of the season, although years of disappointment and the lingering memory of the 1981 collapse made them reluctant to take anything for granted.

Rovers remained top of the table into the New Year with Kilmarnock emerging as their main challengers for the title. The Ayrshire side were not dissimilar to Rovers, playing attractive, passing football under the guidance of a young player-manager, Tommy Burns. The first two league meetings between the teams had been drawn and as the season moved into 1993, Rovers had to travel to Rugby Park twice in January, having been drawn together in the Scottish Cup. Both matches would prove a severe test for the Kirkcaldy side.

On 9 January a large crowd of 7,309 arrived at Rugby Park for the Scottish Cup tie, including a sizeable support from Kirkcaldy. Already trailing from a Bobby Williamson strike after 16 minutes, Rovers suffered a major blow when goalkeeper Tom Carson injured himself and had to be replaced. With no substitute keeper on the bench, Davie Sinclair was forced to take over.

'I was actually quite up for it,' says Sinclair. 'You go in goals in training and you are diving about but then you are on that park in front of six or seven thousand and it is a whole different ball game.'

He was soon picking the ball out of his net when George McCluskey broke into the box and scored. Things got worse minutes later when George McGeachie was beaten for pace by

Porteous and resorted to pulling his shirt to halt his run. With McGeachie having already been booked for an identical foul on Bobby Williamson, the referee had no choice but to send him off.

Rovers headed for the dressing room at half-time 2-0 down, reduced to ten men and with a makeshift goalkeeper. Kilmarnock added three more goals in the second half to win 5-0.

'It was horrendous,' says Sinclair. 'I was getting beat at the near post and with shots that I should never have let in. Everything was squirming through my body.' The defeat was disappointing but an opportunity to atone quickly presented itself with a return to Rugby Park in the league, three weeks later.

As the league match kicked off, there appeared to be unfinished business from the previous game with five bookings in the first half alone. A clash between McCluskey and John McStay on 37 minutes resulted in both players being dismissed.

McStay recounts the incident. 'I remember McCluskey came up for a corner and we had a wee tussle,' he says. 'After the ball went out, I turned and looked about and had a slight dig at him and he chased after me and punched me. I thought I was getting away with it, but the referee sent us both off.'

McStay adds, 'Afterwards in the dressing room, Jimmy Nicholl says to me, "Did you do anything?" and I said, "I never did anything, he just hit me." He says, "Well, I am watching it on TV tomorrow and if you done anything you're getting fined."

'I thought, "Oh Christ!" Fortunately for me, you never saw anything on the TV, so I got away with it.'

The Rovers team were not so lucky as they conceded three late goals to hand Kilmarnock the points. The Raith fans who tuned in to watch the Sunday highlights heard Jim White proclaim, 'Killie now believe they can catch Raith Rovers and go up as champions.'

If the media thought that Nicholl's men would surrender top spot easily, they were mistaken. The manner of the two defeats to Kilmarnock had been damaging but there was a determination in the squad to push on and secure promotion. Rovers continued to dominate the rest of the teams in the division with fast-flowing, attacking football, remaining unbeaten in their next seven games.

Indeed it was Kilmarnock who stuttered, losing three matches and drawing against Cowdenbeath. When the Ayrshire club travelled to Stark's Park on 13 March for the final meeting between the two sides they knew that they had to win to have any chance of catching Rovers in the title race. In front of BBC cameras, covering a game at Stark's Park for the first time since 1969, Rovers all but ended Kilmarnock's championship hopes.

A large crowd of 4,738 watched Rovers comfortably defeat their rivals 2-0. Raith took the lead after 28 minutes when Brewster raced into the box and fired a shot past Bobby Geddes. Any hopes of a Kilmarnock fightback were extinguished in 56 minutes when, just seconds after Gordon Arthur saved a stinging Bobby Williamson shot, Rovers broke and added a second when Dalziel outpaced the Kilmarnock defence to direct the ball home.

It was a goal that would win the Rovers striker £500, a case of champagne and the *Daily Record* Silver Shot title as the second person to reach 30 goals that season, Ally McCoist having already claimed the Golden Shot award.

For the remainder of the game the Rovers support taunted their opponents with suggestions about where they could place their paper roses.

Reflecting on the game later that evening in the *Sportscene* studio, Derek Johnstone was in no doubt what the result meant as he described Rovers as 'an absolute certainty' for promotion.

The manager was more cautious. 'People want me to say yes that's us promoted and they want me to jump the gun, but what I will say is if we get over next week against Dunfermline, then Ayr, then Hamilton. If I get five out of six, the next three games, then I'll say yes,' said Nicholl.

In the end his side only secured four points from the next three games, but a comfortable defeat of Dunfermline and two draws left them on the very brink of the Premier Division. Champagne had been packed on the team bus for the trips to Somerset Park and Douglas Park but had remained unopened. The supporters were less concerned with the arithmetic of promotion and joyfully invaded the pitch at Douglas Park after the 2-2 draw with Hamilton.

Promotion was officially secured against Dumbarton at a sunny Stark's Park in the second week of April. An expectant crowd of almost 5,000 arrived to see Rovers beat Dumbarton

2-0, and, courtesy of a late winner for Clydebank against Dunfermline, clinch the First Division title.

At the final whistle the crowd rushed on to the pitch with a mixture of jubilation and relief. It was glorious chaos as the team was carried off the pitch on the shoulders of fans, with Nicholl sporting a policeman's hat at one point. 'We are the Champions' played over the loudspeaker and the team re-emerged from the directors' box to receive the acclaim of the crowd and spray them with champagne.

'It was a great feeling to win the championship in front of our own support,' says Nicholl, 'and marvellous to see the way the fans rushed on to the field to celebrate at the end. Winning the deciding points at Stark's Park made it all the sweeter.'

When a journalist later pointed out to Nicholl that it was effectively a treble year for him with Raith Rovers, Manchester United and Rangers all winning titles, he quipped, 'When I was a boy in Belfast, I supported Linfield and they have won the Irish League championship, so make that four!'

For the players it was just reward for a remarkable effort. Gordon Dalziel, who had become Rovers' all-time record league goalscorer during the season, recalls an incident in the dressing room after the Dumbarton win that summed up for him why Raith were champions.

'I scored a penalty and they made me retake it because Ian MacLeod had come in to the box,' he says. 'Then I missed it. It was incredible because we had won the league that day and I had a ding-dong with Ian in the dressing room afterwards because he had run into the box. That was how demanding we were of each other.'

The title win was a poignant moment for the striker. 'It was a great feeling to think we had come from the Second Division under Frank to now being in the top league,' says Dalziel. 'It was a long journey.'

The celebrations were just getting started. 'We went up to the Abbotshall Hotel and all the fans were in there,' says John McStay. 'They had to shut the street up as it was just one massive party. I don't think we got to sleep for two days after that. That whole season was winning every week and the atmosphere about the place was superb. There are better players than me in the history of Scottish football who have not won any league medals, so to get my hands on a league medal with Raith Rovers was brilliant.'

Davie Sinclair derived particular pleasure from having edged out rivals Dunfermline in the championship race, 'With me coming from Dunfermline it was nice to get the better of them when we won the championship in 1992/93. I always got a lot of stick playing for Rovers and it was always nice to beat the Pars, particularly having played with them as a youngster. It was sweet revenge.'

The congratulations for the manager and the team started to roll in. Chairman Peter Campsie was fulsome in his praise, 'Two years ago the board took a bit of a gamble when they were persuaded by the manager to authorise full-time football for the club, but I would heartily congratulate Jimmy Nicholl on the success he has achieved.'

He added defiantly, 'People have said we didn't want promotion. That was rubbish. But you only kill these stories by getting there.'

The *Fife Free Press* produced a ten-page souvenir supplement with the simple headline 'We did it!' and local Labour MP Lewis Moonie put forward a motion to the House of Commons congratulating the team.

Rovers fan and author Harry Richie would later devote a chapter to the title win in the appropriately-named book *My Favourite Year* by Nick Hornby.

It was a magnificent personal achievement for Nicholl. In only his second full season as manager he had succeeded where so many others had failed in taking the club into the top division, winning the title with six games to spare and playing a style of football still fondly remembered by every Rovers supporter privileged enough to witness it. He had won many major honours in his playing career but winning as a manager meant more.

'In these games I was a player and only had to think of myself,' he said. 'Now I've had to make decisions and see if they turned out right or wrong. I'm glad it has all paid off.'

As he reflected on the achievement, he felt an enormous sense of pride, but he didn't let himself dwell too long on that emotion. He would be taking his squad to Celtic Park, Ibrox Stadium and Pittodrie. He needed to make sure that they would be ready.

8

BACKWARDS WALK

Glasgow, May 1993

BOB PAXTON sat at the Scottish Football League's Annual
General Meeting waiting to vote on league reconstruction.
His club, Raith Rovers, had just been promoted to the
Premier Division and he was looking forward to the 1993/94
season with eager anticipation.

The proposal before him suggested four divisions of ten teams
ready for the start of 1994/95. It was a change that would make
life more difficult for the Kirkcaldy club as it would mean that
three sides would be relegated from the Premier Division at the
end of the campaign, rather than the usual two, increasing the
likelihood of Rovers making a quick return to the First Division.

The Rovers board was split on the merits of the proposal
but Paxton had left for Glasgow with instructions to vote with
the majority and oppose reconstruction. When the vote finally
came, Paxton ignored his instructions and went in favour of
reconstruction, a move that condemned Raith to almost certain
relegation.

The fact that it was Paxton's vote that had enabled the
reconstruction plans to secure the two-thirds majority necessary
made matters worse. If he had used Rovers' four votes as his board
had wished, it would have been enough to ensure the status quo
was maintained.

Paxton was defiant as he faced reporters. 'I did have a brief from our board but I did what I felt was right,' he said. 'There are some members of the board who will be unhappy tonight.

'Possibly it would have been better for Raith Rovers to have the status quo or a 16-club division, but I took the decision for the benefit of the game as a whole. Perhaps in the short term I have done Raith a disservice but I've done the best thing for the club in the long run.'

Partick Thistle director Brown McMaster was withering in his criticism and described the outcome as 'turkeys voting for Christmas.'

Paxton would later comment, 'I made myself very unpopular with certain people in Kirkcaldy but they do not know the true facts about football.' He left Glasgow knowing that his vote had just made what was always going to be a challenging first season in the Premier Division even more difficult.

Jimmy Nicholl reflects now on the decision and the impact it had on his hopes for the season. 'For whatever reason, Bob was put in the position he was,' says Nicholl. 'He was told, "Don't be voting for that; don't be voting for that," but he must have been put under pressure or whatever. I don't know the real story. All I knew as a football man, three were to go down, which was 25 per cent of the league and we had to finish fourth bottom. It was always going to be difficult.'

Rovers started the season with the squad more or less intact from the previous campaign. The squad had enjoyed a trip to Magaluf over the summer as a reward for their title win and had been delighted to discover that the Falkirk squad, the team they were replacing in the Premier Division, shared the same flight and hotel. 'We gave them dog's abuse,' laughs Gordon Dalziel.

The one disappointment had been the loss of striker Craig Brewster to Dundee United. Brewster left with fond memories of his time in Kirkcaldy. 'Sometimes things are meant to be and my time at Raith Rovers was meant to be. I just loved every minute of it,' he says.

Nicholl had placed his faith in the players who had taken the club into the Premier Division. 'It was a case of what do you do now that you are up?' he says. 'Do you give the boys a chance to play in the Premier Division after they have worked that hard or do you have a clear-out and deny them that chance? I thought, "I am going to give these boys an opportunity." They had earned it.'

At the first game of the season against St Johnstone, the manager wrote in his programme notes, 'This is the day we have all been looking forward to: the arrival of Premier League football in Kirkcaldy with the prospect of visits from Rangers, Celtic, Aberdeen and all the rest of Scotland's leading clubs.'

He went on, 'We are still a small club compared to many in the top league and our resources are correspondingly smaller also. This will be a new experience for me and for every single player in our team. We know it is going to be a very difficult season but we will give it a real go!'

Rovers certainly gave it a go but found life in the Premier Division difficult. In the early part of the season they struggled to find wins and were on the end of a number of bruising 4-1 defeats. The loss of Brewster and his prolific partnership with Dalziel was a blow for the Kirkcaldy side with one reporter noting in an early draw with Partick, 'Raith Rovers have settled well into their Premier Division adventure, although the need to replace Craig Brewster was glaring, with the veteran Dalziel still laying the ball off to the spaces where Brewster no longer is.'

As the season progressed Rovers remained competitive but were still finding it difficult to secure wins. Nicholl's determination to persist with the flowing football that saw his side stroll to the First Division championship won plenty of admirers but few points.

Nicholl reflects on the early-season form of the team. 'In the early stages we went through something of a learning process and at times were perhaps a bit naive and got punished for it,' he says.

Davie Sinclair recalls how challenging the step up to the Premier Division was for the players. 'It was really hard in the Premier at first,' he says. 'It is a totally different level of fitness and you are playing against better players. You are playing teams like Motherwell and you think you can get a result but they have been there a long time and they know how to grind out a result. It was a bit of a culture shock.'

Rovers were still winning praise for their attacking style but results continued to frustrate.

'We were getting great press at the time but I remember Jimmy saying, "Hard luck stories, hard luck stories; I am fed up hearing hard luck stories,"' says Stevie Crawford.

As they reached the end of the year, Rovers had registered just four wins; two against Dundee and two against Hearts. The players and supporters were enjoying visits to Ibrox, Parkhead, Tynecastle and Pittodrie but a lack of victories against fellow relegation contenders left the club second bottom of the Premier Division.

John McStay believes that their commitment to attacking football worked against them. 'I think a lot of it was that Jimmy just didn't change his style,' he says. 'We just kept going for goals. I remember that Kilmarnock got promoted with us and Tommy Burns changed his style to try and stay up.'

He adds, 'We played some good football in the Premier League. I think everybody who watched us enjoyed us that season.'

The team were hindered by the loss of influential midfielder Peter Hetherston to injury. 'I picked up a lower abdominal injury which kept me out for three or four months and I had to miss a lot of important games in the Premier League,' says Hetherston.

Sitting on the sidelines while the club struggled to adapt to life in the top division was not easy for the Rovers captain.

'I had more fall-outs with the physio than anyone else,' he recalls. 'Gerry Docherty was a gentleman but he had a hard time with me. I smashed his doors, stomped out of his room and put the phone down on him. I came back probably a wee bit early because I was desperate to help the lads out as they were struggling a bit.'

Nicholl attempted to strengthen his squad with the signing of striker Ally Graham from Motherwell and goalkeeper Scott Thomson from Forfar, in a move that saw Gordon Arthur leave Stark's Park to join the Angus club. Graham was a traditional target man who could win headers and hold up the ball but was struggling under Tommy McLean, who preferred a lone striker system.

'I will be honest. I didn't enjoy my football at all under wee Tam,' says Graham. 'I would be driving up Airbles Road and as soon as I saw that Motorola Stand I just thought, "Oh no." He would persist with playing one up front and he tried to change my game but at 27 there was no way that was going to happen. No way.

'Tommy called me into the office and said, "Jimmy Nicholl is interested. Do you want to go and talk to him?" I knew that Jimmy had been watching me when I was at Ayr United and I'd always known that he had quite liked me. I said, "Well if I am not getting a chance here, then it is probably the best thing to do."

'I didn't have any hesitation. The pull for me was I knew a few guys playing there already. I knew Dalziel, McStay, Hetherston and Ronnie Coyle. That was a big attraction. I thought if I am going to be travelling with these guys then that is something to look forward to.'

He was initially uncertain about whether he had made the right decision but he quickly discovered that the atmosphere at Stark's Park suited his own exuberant personality.

'I had played in Kirkcaldy with Ayr a few times but when I saw the old ground I thought, "Jesus, what have I done?"' he says. 'At first I was thinking, "What am I doing here?" but they made me welcome right from the start and the training was brilliant and I started to enjoy my football again.'

It was a world away from life at Fir Park under McLean. 'It was like you were never allowed to talk to anyone at Motherwell and there was a kind of fear,' he recalls. 'It was a totally different sort of camaraderie at Rovers. Jimmy Nicholl encouraged us to socialise and we did most of our socialising in Kirkcaldy. I think Jimmy thought that was the way it should be. The fact that the strip had Jackie O's nightclub on it, that summed it up. The team spirit was fantastic.'

Graham was soon introduced to the slightly unorthodox way of doing things at the Kirkcaldy club.

'The first time I went up to stay in Kirkcaldy before the game on the Saturday, the boys took me to the Valente fish and chip shop for a fish supper,' he says. 'I would never eat fish and chips before a game normally but that was my introduction to life at Raith Rovers.'

Goalkeeper Thomson was less of an extrovert than Graham but also proved a strong addition to the squad. Thomson had been at Dundee United for seven years in a strong squad that reached the UEFA Cup Final against IFK Gothenburg in 1987. His first-team opportunities had been limited to only six starts so he moved to Forfar and was part-time when the approach came from Rovers.

'I was working in a bar, working in a sports shop and I had been through three stages of the fire brigade,' he recalls. 'I got a phone call one night at 11 o'clock and it was my manager at Forfar. He told me I was to phone Jimmy Nicholl and that was the first of me knowing anything about it. I phoned Jimmy, then the clubs agreed a fee and I played one last game for Forfar before I came to Stark's Park. I was really excited and couldn't wait to join the team.'

It was not Thomson's first time in Kirkcaldy, having made a single loan appearance for Raith Rovers in a 3-2 defeat to Stranraer in the 1985/86 season. Like Graham, he found the atmosphere at Stark's Park a welcome change from his previous experience of full-time football under Jim McLean at Dundee United.

'It was a good environment to come in to,' he says. 'They had just been promoted and they trusted each other and they trusted the manager. It was quite a tight-knit group, with a good team spirit. Jimmy Nicholl was a breath of fresh air in terms of his enthusiasm. He put so much into it and he just seemed to get the best out of players.

'To go from Forfar to playing in the Premier Division at Ibrox and Parkhead was a massive leap for me but it was always big games and that builds up your confidence.'

In his first interview for the Rovers match programme Thomson was asked his thoughts on the art of saving a penalty.

He replied, 'I watch penalty kicks being taken on the telly, so I can get an idea of the tactics used. Penalties are a pretty hit and miss affair. I suppose a lot of it comes down to luck. I'd say on average I could probably save about one out of every five.'

The Rovers fans would have to wait a little longer until they would be able to judge whether the average he claimed was accurate.

If Rovers were finding life difficult on the field, then a combination of ground redevelopment, a higher wage bill and bad weather conspired to make it challenging off the field.

The club were struggling to cope with the cost of life in the Premier Division with reports at the time suggesting they were over £300,000 in the red. The loss of fixtures and income over the Christmas period brought matters to a head. Some in the boardroom had proposed a new flotation to raise additional funds for the club but a number of stockholders resisted the idea.

Shortly after New Year, 61-year-old Peter Campsie resigned as chairman, saying that he was sacrificing himself in the hope of persuading reluctant stockholders into agreeing to a new flotation.

He told the *Fife Free Press*, 'Due to the present financial position of the club, and due to the present position of the team in the Premier Division, I have stood down as chairman and honorary club secretary. As chairman, I was under great pressure to redevelop the stadium to meet Lord Justice Taylor's requirements and this has put a heavy burden on the club's finances. I hope my action will bring closer my desire for a new share issue, which is well overdue.'

Two days after Campsie's departure, Bob Paxton also resigned. Paxton had found life difficult after his vote on league reconstruction and he said that he found it impossible to work with certain individuals. The vacant seats on the Stark's Park board were taken by local builder Alex Penman and John Lister, an accountant and club historian.

The board released a statement to try and reassure supporters which said, 'The club has been the subject of many articles in the press over the past two weeks, of a type which would not be of our choosing. The press headlines of "crisis" and "turmoil" are misplaced. The much publicised "financial problems" of the club have been quantified as being presently manageable. The day-to-day operation of the club is ongoing and has not been disrupted.'

The resignation of Campsie paved the way for an extension of the share capital, which was finally agreed in mid-April. After much discussion, Raith Rovers FC Holdings was formed, with the supporters' club agreeing to transfer most of their shares in the football club to the new company, effectively giving Penman control of Raith Rovers.

The move would stabilise the finances of the club, allowing them to remain full-time, but left the ownership of the club in one person's hands, a move which would have lasting repercussions for the club in future years.

On the field, results continued to disappoint, even if the praise from journalists continued to come. One wrote, 'In a division where they have too much hash and bash, Raith's more cultured approach, despite their lowly position, is to be admired.'

Right-back Stephen McAnespie, who had been at Aberdeen, and midfielder Danny Lennon from Hibernian were added to the squad.

'I saw wee Danny playing for Hibs' reserves,' says Nicholl. 'He was just coming back from a broken leg but he was all over the pitch. You couldn't get near him. I said to Alex Miller, "If you are ever getting rid of him let me know." He said, "You can have him Jimmy", so I signed him.'

Lennon's arrival couldn't prevent the club from suffering the seemingly inevitable fate of relegation. On 26 April, Rovers took their last gulp of air in the Premier Division as they were officially relegated after a 1-1 draw with Hibernian. Former Rover Keith Wright scored the goal that confirmed his old club's return to the First Division.

Scott Thomson believes that a failure to win games against relegation rivals cost the Kirkcaldy club.

'We weren't a million miles away,' says the goalkeeper. 'We were a bit unfortunate. We used to do really well in home games against Celtic and Rangers but games which we really needed to win, we either lost or drew.'

Ronnie Coyle felt that the club had been ill-equipped for the demands of the top division. 'It was as if they were playing at it,' he says. 'There was a lot of naivety, and I don't think we were geared up off the field to make as much as we could have done out of the whole experience.'

He adds, 'The players enjoyed it. Although we lost heavily to the bigger teams, we always knew that we were better than most of the teams in the division, although we didn't get the results.'

There remained a sense of pride around the club at how they had performed in their first Premier Division experience, even if it hadn't been enough to extend their stay beyond one season.

'You couldn't help but enjoy the Premier,' says midfielder Colin Cameron. 'All the hard work that had went on to get the club to that position, it was an adventure for fans and players. We just loved playing in the Premier League; playing against the calibre of players we were; having Rangers and Celtic coming to Stark's Park on a regular basis. It was great for the club and the town.'

The season was to end in relative farce due to an incident when Rovers visited Ibrox in April. The match ended in a routine 4-0 win for the Glasgow side but a clash between Rangers centre-forward Duncan Ferguson and Rovers' John McStay after 33 minutes dominated the headlines.

McStay recounts the event. 'I remember it well,' he says. 'The ball got put in the corner and I turned and took the ball and he pulled me back. He never said anything but just as I turned round he banged me.'

Ferguson had headbutted the full-back. Astoundingly, in what journalist Kevin McCarra would later describe as a 'deplorable act of leniency', referee Kenny Clark failed to produce a card and contented himself with a few words of admonition to the player.

The SFA were not as forgiving and summoned Ferguson and McStay to an SFA committee meeting. Initially, the Ibrox club had advised their striker not to attend because he had already been charged with assault in connection with the alleged incident, but when they realised that Ferguson could face suspension from the Scottish Cup Final for non-attendance, they relented. At Stark's Park confusion reigned.

'Rovers told me that Rangers had told them Ferguson wasn't turning up so we didn't need to go,' says McStay. 'I was playing golf on the Tuesday with Peter and somebody phoned me saying, "You were supposed to be at a meeting." Ferguson had turned up.'

The non-appearance of the Rovers player irritated the SFA chief executive Jim Farry. From the steps of the association's headquarters in Park Gardens he voiced his frustration with the Kirkcaldy club.

'They were given unambiguous advice about the need for John McStay to appear today,' he said. 'It is entirely possible they and the player could be fined or suspended. It is entirely possible Raith might be suspended from playing their final league match against Dundee United on Saturday.'

Rovers were effectively barred from Scottish football. When Stevie Crawford was selected for a Scotland under-21 international, the SFA press release indicated that he would only travel if the suspension was lifted. The meeting was hastily rearranged and the suspension removed.

'They rescheduled it for the Thursday and Penman and Nicholl picked me up and took me down to that,' says McStay. 'I had to go in and sit at the big table and Ferguson was sitting next to us. It was all about Rangers. It was really nothing to do with us.'

If the defender thought the incident would be quickly forgotten, he was mistaken. Ferguson was on a suspended sentence for other violent incidents and the assault on McStay was classed as a breach of his conditions, resulting in the Rangers player being handed a custodial punishment.

The fact that Ferguson was being jailed for other offences and not the assault on McStay was frequently overlooked in the press coverage and with family connections to rivals Celtic, McStay became a target for the Rangers fans' ire. The unwanted attention began to have an effect on the Rovers player.

'Jock went through a wee bad time of it with that incident but he came through it,' says Gordon Dalziel. 'He has great character. He was a very, very underestimated footballer and a massive part of Raith Rovers.'

McStay now views the controversy surrounding the incident as the beginning of the end for his Raith Rovers career. 'I felt as if the club let me down a bit when that happened,' he says.

Over the summer, contract negotiations between the player and the club stalled. 'I did the pre-season with them,' says McStay. 'I played all the games and Penman was supposed to be bringing the contract over to Ireland to sign, but it kept getting put off and put off. Then the Friday before the start of the season Jimmy freed me.'

He describes the moments after he found out he was no longer a Raith Rovers player as the worst of his career. 'Jimmy took all the players that were playing Saturday on to the park to discuss the game. I just went in the dressing room and changed. It broke my heart walking out the door to my car. I just sat in the motor, waiting on the boys: Daz, Ronnie and Ally Graham. I was driving us home and I couldn't even speak to them. I didn't tell them in the car what had happened but they knew something was up. By the time I got from Kirkcaldy to the Forth Road Bridge it came over the radio that Raith Rovers had just released me.'

The defender suspects that the fall-out from the Ferguson incident played a part in the decision to release him, but regardless of whether it had or not, Rovers had lost a much-loved character from the dressing room.

McStay reflects on his time at Kirkcaldy and feels that the experience he had at Raith Rovers was the best of his career. 'After I left I wasn't the same player because it was as if I had left my home,' he says. 'I had left the place that I loved, and I just couldn't settle anywhere else. I compared everywhere I went with Rovers and my heart wasn't in it.'

An eventful year in the Premier Division had ended in failure as Rovers had failed to secure their place in the top division but the fact that they had continued to play good football and tried to entertain meant that the players, supporters and manager had enjoyed the experience.

The board of directors had announced that funding was in place to ensure the club would remain full-time for the next two seasons, irrespective of the division in which they played. Nicholl knew that his side were still a good team and the young talent in his squad now had an extra year's experience.

They would just have to recharge, regroup and go again.

9

SMELLS LIKE TEAM SPIRIT
North Queensferry, August 1993

GORDON DALZIEL sat in the front seat of the car travelling back through to the west of Scotland with his Rovers team-mates. He was in a particularly good mood as not only had they spent the day playing golf, but he had managed to win and claim the prize of a brand new Pringle golf jumper.

On the return journey he was making sure that his travelling companions, especially Ronnie Coyle, knew exactly how pleased he was at the new addition to his wardrobe.

'We were all travelling back after I had won at golf,' recalls Dalziel. 'I was really rubbing it in with Ronnie because I knew he hated to lose. I was going on about the Pringle I had won as a prize as we were driving over the Forth Road Bridge and he asked to see it. Ronnie said he was thinking about buying one for himself.'

Dalziel handed the jumper to Coyle, who wound down the car window and threw it out. 'I never saw it again!' says Dalziel.

It was typical of the competitive spirit in the Rovers squad. There was a strong will to win and determination throughout the team. It was what drove the team on to be successful.

'I remember Barry Wilson came to Rovers and in the first half I was playing up front and he was playing wide right,' says

Dalziel. 'I walked in at half-time and I walked over to him and said, "Listen you arsehole, see when you get down the wing, you put the ball in the box. See if you put the ball in the box, I will score goals."

'That was just the way we were. We were demanding of each other from three o'clock to quarter to five on a Saturday. You knew you'd better make those runs and you'd better get that ball in the box. That is why we were successful.'

Defender Stephen McAnespie agrees, 'You had to maintain your standards because there were others guys waiting to get your job. You never took anything for granted. I was fighting for the rest of my career and I wanted to be the best that I could be, every game. There was no complacency.'

The training schedule that Nicholl devised for the squad copied an unorthodox but successful routine he had experienced at Manchester United.

Nicholl explains how it worked, 'If you won on the Saturday, you were off Sunday. You were off on a Monday. You trained hard Tuesday, played golf on a Wednesday, warm-up and five-a-side on a Thursday and five-a-side on a Friday. As unprofessional as it sounds, that is what we did at Raith Rovers.'

The routine worked and bonded the squad into a cohesive unit on and off the pitch. 'I think it worked because boys respected Jimmy,' says striker Stevie Crawford. 'We knew that Sunday was your day of recovery and he was giving you the Monday off but you looked after yourself and on a Tuesday it was work. On a Tuesday, the boys knew they were coming into a hard, hard session.

'We all believed in it. If you were left out of Jimmy's team, it was all the usual stuff but not once in my time did I ever hear anybody say, "Oh I have had enough of this. I am wanting away." You believed in him.'

The space his unorthodox training routine left for socialising and activities was viewed as critical for Nicholl as it helped knit the team together into a proper unit who were prepared to work for each other on a Saturday.

'We were all pretty close,' says Colin Cameron. 'We tended to mix together outside the football and became not just team-mates, but friends as well. That helps as you get a bond and you start helping each other out, on and off the field. When you are in a game and one of your team-mates is not doing well, then you are prepared to be there and muck in and help them out and get them through the situation.

'We had this team spirit, togetherness, mentality that whatever happened, we were going to stick together and if things weren't quite going our way, we were going to get through it and come out the other side. You can't coach that. You have got to have the right players for that to happen and Jimmy had the right players.'

The team spirit was helped by the fact that most of the younger players in the team were local and had come through the ranks of Fife football. At the heart of this group were Shaun Dennis and Davie Sinclair, two uncompromising characters on and off the pitch.

Dennis had broken into the first team at the start of 1988/89 in a pre-season friendly against Rangers at Stark's Park. He was a big, rugged, no-nonsense centre-half who seemed mature beyond his years.

'I remember playing a practice match against big Shaun,' says Dalziel. 'I saw this boy who just had no fear. He didn't care who you were, he would just get in about you and I thought, "He's got a fantastic talent."'

Frank Connor had been impressed by the raw talent of the youngster and quickly gave Dennis an opportunity in the senior squad. 'Big Shaun was the best,' says Connor. 'I love the big guy. I wanted to boot his arse sometimes but Shaun Dennis would have died for me.'

By the start of the 1990s, Dennis had made the number five shirt at Stark's Park his domain. He was ambitious and in his first player profile for the match programme he spoke of his desire to reach the 'highest position possible' in the game.

He won his first under-21 cap in a 3-0 win for Scotland in Switzerland in 1991 and there was speculation that Liam Brady might sign him for Celtic. The former miner was a fanatical Celtic fan and would have welcomed a move to his boyhood club but it never materialised and he continued to impress at Stark's Park. He became a firm favourite of the supporters with his strength and his willingness to throw himself into challenges.

'Shaun was a great player,' says Jason Dair. 'He could have played for the top teams, no problem. He read the game well, was good on the ball and was hard as nails. He was fast too, and he used to challenge boys to races over half a park. Once he got going, he was very fast and I think only Barry Wilson and Stevie Crawford managed to beat him.'

If there was a weakness in the young defender's game then it was his ongoing struggle with his weight.

'Shaun Dennis would have been a Scotland player if he could have controlled his weight,' says Ronnie Coyle. 'He came back one pre-season weighing 16 stone. I always had a weight problem and thought 13 and a half or 14 stone was far too heavy but Shaun came back at 16 stone! Too fond of the drink, curries and so on, but a great player.

'If only he had screwed the head on when he was getting recognition, got his weight down and kept it off. Shaun would have got a Scotland call-up out of it.'

Playing alongside Dennis was fellow Fifer David Sinclair. 'Sinky' was slightly older than his team-mate but reached the first team slightly later, during the 1990/91 season. Sinclair was from Dunfermline and had been with the Kirkcaldy club's rivals as a youth.

'I was 12 years old when Dunfermline came in for me,' says Sinclair. 'I was playing for High Valleyfield Youth Club and I was attached to Dunfermline until I was 18. I won the BP Youth Cup with them and we played Rangers in the quarter-finals. They had all the big names: Nesbitt, Spencer, McSwegan but we beat them 3-0.'

The success did not guarantee a contract and, along with many of his team-mates, Sinclair was released by the Pars. 'I made one appearance for the first team in a friendly and not long afterwards Leishman told me that he had to let me go,' he recalls. 'It's a heart-breaking moment in your life.'

Sinclair had offers from junior football but decided to persist in his attempts to secure a senior club. 'I had been farmed out to Dunfermline Jubilee when I was with Dunfermline and they kept phoning me to go back but I didn't like the juniors. I said to them, "I am not coming back. I am going to the under-21s." They said, "You'll never make a football player."'

Sinclair smiles, 'I think I was about nine or ten weeks with Kelty under-21s and then I was signed by Raith Rovers.'

It could have easily been a case of what might have been for Rovers as immediately prior to signing with the Kirkcaldy club, Sinclair had been interesting Hearts.

'I actually went on trial with Hearts before I signed with Raith Rovers,' says Sinclair. 'I was working with Craig Levein, who had started his own electrical business and was helping install alarms all over Scotland. I had to stop training with Hearts during the week because of work but I was still playing under-21s on a Saturday and someone came to watch me from Raith Rovers and the next thing "bang", I had signed.'

Sinclair arrived in Kirkcaldy and immediately got to work under Frank Connor. 'Frank was hard but fair,' recalls Sinclair. 'He was a really good one-to-one person and very thorough in what he did. His knowledge of the game was fantastic and at training he would take you aside and tell you "do this or do that". He was strict though and if you did something wrong then he didn't miss you.'

There was no doubt that Sinclair was a talented footballer but some had concerns about his temperament. Andy Harrow, the former Rovers player and reserve-team coach, who worked with Sinclair at the time, recalls his attitude.

'Sinky was a bit rough-and-ready and I thought that would be his downfall,' says Harrow. 'He was always getting booked for the wrong things, getting involved in some stupid things, but he was definitely a talented player.'

For many of the Rovers support, this rough-and-ready approach was exactly what they loved. At times he felt like their representative on the pitch with his commitment, determination and willingness to battle for the team. Together Sinclair and Dennis provided Rovers with a formidable and fearless core.

'As one of the younger ones in the team, it was great to have the likes of Shaun and Sinky on hand,' says Jason Dair. 'You know they were always there if there was any bother. This was also the case off the field!'

Away from the pitch the team bonded and developed a tremendous team spirit. 'The whole unit was bonded together and it was a great squad to be in at the time,' says Ronnie Coyle.

'There was no bitching and no arguing and everyone had a good night out every few weeks. It was the best social life I have ever experienced, and that's how we thrived, because we knew how to enjoy ourselves off the field and we went on to the park to enjoy ourselves too.'

For Dalziel, the togetherness of the squad was a key ingredient in the success of the club. 'People always ask why Raith were so successful back then,' he says. 'I think it had a lot to do with the people we had in the dressing room at that time.

'Dressing rooms are what contribute to a good side and at Raith we had some good characters in there: Jock McStay and Peter Hetherston and all these guys and the likes of big Ally Graham. He was a really funny boy, especially in the car driving up.

'You would often lose characters, Peter Hetherston for instance, when he went to Aberdeen, but you always seemed to get characters in to replace the ones who had left. That was our strength and we took it from there on to the park.'

The Kirkcaldy dressing room was no place for shrinking violets as it became a home for incessant goading and wind-ups. Most football clubs have one or two jokers but Raith Rovers seemed to have a whole dressing room of them.

Danny Lennon found it far removed from his previous experience at Hibs. 'I joined Rovers from Hibs, where the set-up was very professional,' he says. 'Things were done differently at Raith. I've never known a dressing room like it for wind-ups.'

The atmosphere around the club produced many comic moments. One such incident was when Stark's Park was broken into during a reserve game.

Dalziel laughs as he recounts the story. 'Peter Hetherston and I had just come back from injury and we were playing Rangers in a reserve game on a Monday night,' he says. 'We walked in to the dressing room after the game and my suit was away. I started slaughtering Peter for it as I thought he had stolen my suit, but then we looked at his peg and his suit was away too!

'Someone had left the window open and someone had come in and taken the suits. We only had our shoes and our tracksuits and we couldn't drive back down the road either as Peter's keys had been in his suit jacket pocket.'

The police were called and they told the players that they would keep a watch on Hetherston's car overnight.

'We were staying at the Abbotshall Hotel so we had someone coming up the next day with spare keys for his car, with it being one of the sponsored cars,' says Dalziel. 'We were walking towards the ground with our dress shoes and tracksuits on and I said to him, "I'd piss myself if we walked around the corner and your car was away." We got around the corner and it was. Whoever stole his suit had come back for the car!'

Hetherston recalls Dalziel's excitement on discovering the theft, 'We got round the corner and Daz breaks into a sprint and he starts jumping up and down shouting, "It's stolen; it's stolen. They've come back for it." To make it worse it was four Rangers supporters that had stolen it.'

The team bonded on nights out and pre-season trips to Northern Ireland, where the emphasis was as much on socialising as it was on playing football. 'The minute we had played the game, Jimmy would stop the bus and get some cans of Guinness saying, "There you go boys",' recalls Dalziel.

'The banter and the fun were just terrific,' says Julian Broddle. 'That was the great thing about Raith. Jimmy Nic knew how to get the best out of guys who were at the end of their careers; young lads who were just starting up; free transfers and home-grown lads. He could blend them by having nights out or taking us to Ireland or just letting us off the leash now and again.

'I think he was happy to allow us to do that because he knew that it was building up this team bonding. Jimmy did tell us to calm it down a few times but I think behind closed doors he was probably thinking "brilliant".'

For the younger players, the dressing room could be an intimidating place at first but they were quickly accepted as part of the team and included in the banter.

'The jokes in the dressing room were unreal,' says Stephen McAnespie. 'Every day it was a battle to get into training and to get away from training. It was every man for himself and you had to become a man quickly, believe me.'

Jason Dair agrees. 'It was a scary place for us young ones and at first we only went near the first-team dressing room if it was really needed,' says Dair. 'There were some great characters in the dressing room and that was the greatest thing about that team, in my opinion. We had a good team but the dressing room and spirit was great.

'We used to socialise as a team, not just one or two, but most of the team would meet up after a game on a Saturday. The stories would then be told through the week about what happened at the weekend and this bond and spirit that we had definitely helped us.'

It would take the experience of subsequent dressing rooms for the young midfielder to fully realise just how special the atmosphere at Stark's Park was.

'When that is your first taste of full-time football, you think that the good players, manager and dressing room banter that we had is what it's like at every club,' he says. 'As you get older, and experience different teams and situations, you realise just how lucky you were and what a special time in your life that was. Every time we manage to get together now it pretty much is still the same. We all still get along and throw abuse at each other as we did back then.'

For Stevie Crawford it was an incredible experience to be in a dressing room like that as a young player. 'I can remember as a young boy just sitting there with my mouth open listening to Daz giving people stick,' he says. 'I can't say enough about the Gordon Dalziels and Ally Grahams of this world: Coylie, Peter Hetherston, Jock McStay. They were all great guys. Even people like Ian MacLeod, an intelligent guy, but he was a big part of winding people up.

'You would come in on the morning and there was always somebody getting wound up and there was stuff happening, childish stuff, but it lifted the dressing room mood. Boys like Sinky and Robbie Raeside used to be the butt of all the jokes but nobody ever took offence and nothing was getting broke, not on purpose anyway! We had respect for Raith Rovers and we had respect for the badge.'

Nicholl was happy to indulge the players a little and enjoyed the atmosphere his squad had created. 'If you liked a laugh and a joke then it was ideal,' he says. 'You had to be on your toes with Dalziel and Ronnie and all those boys. Once you gave as good as you got and you were dishing it out, then it didn't matter. I was quite happy with the banter and the craic as long as they were working hard.'

The infectious team spirit was taken into the dressing room on a Saturday. 'You would walk into our dressing room at two o'clock and you would think these boys are not going to play fitba', says Dalziel. 'There was just hilarious laughing and slagging.'

The squad had a ghetto blaster in the dressing room and it was a race to get there first on a Saturday to be able to choose the music. Nicholl believed it was a great way to remove the pressure from his players. 'It took the pressure off them having to talk or having to try to be funny or do something. It would take their mind off the game,' he says.

The laughs were important but there was also a serious side to Nicholl, who worked tirelessly to instil a self-belief into each player and the squad as a whole. 'Ten minutes before the game, that was when the music got switched off and that was when the serious heads came on,' recalls Jason Dair.

The manager, through his football knowledge and enthusiasm for the game, managed to motivate and cajole his team into giving their best.

'He was still a young man and it was just his enthusiasm,' says Julian Broddle. 'He wanted you to play the right way and he wanted you to be enthusiastic. He was always happy to mix when there was a bit of fun on the training field but when it was time to become the manager, he became the manager and you always knew at which point he was being the boss and you took him seriously.

'We were like one big family. We all relied on each other. No one thought they were better than anyone else and it just clicked. We just went out thinking, "We can win" and it was just about how many goals we were going to get. It was an amazing experience to have that confidence.'

Scott Thomson agrees, 'Jimmy made everyone feel they could beat anybody. He always gave you the belief that you could do anything, individually and as a team.'

Stevie Crawford believes that the manager's enthusiasm stretched far beyond football. 'Jimmy is just a special, special man,' he says. 'He has got that determination about him to be successful. The enthusiasm he has not just for football, but for life in general. He always puts a smile on somebody's face.'

Nicholl was confident that the team spirit he had fostered would allow them to bounce back from the disappointment of relegation. What he didn't know at the time was that, within a matter of months, his Raith Rovers team would embark on an incredible journey that would make history.

10

MEMORIES CAN'T WAIT

Dingwall, August 1994

COLIN CAMERON collected a pass from Davie Kirkwood and made space for himself just outside the Ross County penalty area. He glanced towards the goal and fired a shot past the County goalkeeper and into the net. After a battling 55 minutes from the Highland side, Rovers had finally broken their resistance. Raith led 1-0 and their 1994 League Cup campaign was up and running.

Ten minutes later Cameron was involved again as he sent in a corner for Ally Graham to send a looping header into the net. Dalziel made it three, and two late goals from Graham to complete his hat-trick secured a comfortable 5-0 win and a place in the third round.

'At that time Ross County was an unknown and we were expected to go up there and win,' says Cameron. 'These places are never easy but we had that confidence about us that we were going to try and see how far we could go, and if it meant going up to places like that and getting results, then that is what we would do.'

Graham was delighted with his hat-trick and on the journey back to Fife he let his team-mates know it. 'The main reason I remember Ross County so much is that unfortunately it was a long journey and Ally Graham scored a hat-trick,' says Colin Cameron. 'All we heard for two and a half hours was Ally going on about his hat-trick and how good it was.'

Cameron grew up in Kirkcaldy so it was extra special for him to be playing for Raith Rovers. From an early age the young striker's weekends were dominated by football. 'I was always playing in some team or other,' says Cameron. 'In fact, I very rarely got to see a Rovers match when I was young because I was too busy playing football myself.'

As a boy, he trained with Dundee United for a few months but when an offer was not forthcoming, he returned to Fife to play for Savoy Thistle. It was there he was scouted by Raith Rovers.

'I was 15 when I signed as a schoolboy,' the midfielder recalls. 'Frank Connor was the manager. He ruled with an iron rod. I wouldn't say the younger players were scared of him but he was the type of character who was strong and I think that helped us. You learnt how to respect your manager, the coaches and the experienced players. Frank liked to see how the younger ones were getting on and be involved from time to time. It was great for us because it showed how committed he was to the club.'

Cameron lived near the stadium so the journey to training was short. 'My dad still stays in the same house in Links Street and it was two minutes' walk and I was at the stadium,' he says. 'I was very fortunate that I didn't have to travel. I didn't have that to worry about, so I could really focus on trying to achieve what I wanted to do.'

Cameron would progress steadily through the ranks with the encouragement of his father. He had a number of spells out on loan including a defining period in Ireland with Sligo Rovers.

'I was 17 at the time and I think Jimmy had wanted me to gain experience,' recalls Cameron. 'He felt that going over to Ireland would help me. He stressed to me that it was part of my development and it would improve me as a player.

'We had a player Damien Dunleavy, who was from Sligo and I ended up staying with his parents. Initially it was for a month, and then it got extended to the end of their season, so it was about ten weeks in total.'

Cameron would learn a valuable lesson in his time in Ireland. 'My first game, I was a substitute,' he explains. 'I came on and the first time I got the ball the centre-half absolutely smashed me. It made me realise that I had to move the ball quickly. Probably that one tackle changed my whole outlook on things. When I came back from there, I came back more streetwise and better for the experience.'

He returned to Kirkcaldy, but at the end of that season was concerned that his chances of becoming a professional footballer were receding.

'I remember speaking to my father that season and starting to think about what else I could do,' says Cameron. 'I didn't feel that things were going great. I just got the feeling I wasn't going to be offered another contract.

'My dad just said, "Get your head down and keep working hard and you will get the breaks."'

Jimmy Nicholl decided to try the youngster out in midfield, rather than in his usual position of striker.

'There were about three or four reserve games left of the season and he shuffled me back into midfield and said, "I want to see how you get on there,"' recalls Cameron. 'I wasn't too sure at the time, because I had always been a striker. I was a wee bit pessimistic but I respected Jimmy so I thought, "Let's see how it goes," and I enjoyed it. Looking back, that was probably the turning point in my career. I think I earned myself another year because of those three games.'

He reflects back now and considers what a significant impact that decision made, 'Had Jimmy not put me in midfield I might not have been there the following season and who knows what would have happened to the rest of my life.'

Nicholl included Cameron in the build-up to the 1992/93 season, playing him in friendlies and in the two-day Fife Cup tournament at Bayview. The young midfielder scored in the 3-1 semi-final win over hosts East Fife and netted the winner in the final against Dunfermline the following day. When fellow youth player Jason Dair made his debut against St Mirren a few days later, it motivated Cameron to push for the first team.

'Jason was first and it showed me and Craw that Jimmy would be prepared to put the youngsters in and give them their opportunity,' he says. 'It gave us a focus on what we had to do to get that opportunity.'

Cameron would feature a number of times as a substitute that season before finally making his league debut for Raith Rovers on 26 January 1993 in a 4-2 win over Clydebank at Stark's Park. He performed well and played the full 90 minutes but he couldn't quite match the feat of Dair and Crawford by scoring on his debut. He would have to wait a month before his first league goal arrived in a 2-0 away win at Cowdenbeath.

Cameron became a regular in the team as they won promotion, proving his worth with tremendous energy and skill.

'Colin Cameron was like a machine,' says former team-mate Jason Rowbotham. 'His work rate and his ability to get from box to box were phenomenal. He covered every blade of grass and he could finish as well.'

Julian Broddle agrees. 'You could tell Mickey Cameron was going to be brilliant,' he says. 'You wouldn't say it to him of course but you knew he was going to be an outstanding player. I always thought he could have been brilliant for somebody like Manchester United or that sort of club. He had the ability to do it and he was as good as that in my opinion.'

Ross County had performed well despite the five-goal defeat and manager Bobby Wilson had enjoyed the game against his former employers. He described his team as beaten but not disgraced and reflected ruefully on a chance just before half-time, when the match was still goalless.

'If MacPherson had slotted that one home just before the turn it could have been all so different,' he said, 'but that's football.'

The draw for the third round paired Rovers with old foes Kilmarnock, who, unlike Raith, had managed to survive in the Premier Division the previous season. Nicholl was upbeat about the chance to cross swords with the Ayrshire club again.

'It will suit us down to the ground,' he said. 'We're guaranteed a big crowd so that's some coppers for the board, and we've also a great chance of going through. We've had some good games against Kilmarnock in the past two years and the atmosphere should be great.'

Away from the League Cup the Rovers squad was still trying to adjust to life back in the First Division. Most teams who are relegated suffer an initial hangover and Rovers were no different.

'I was looking at them saying, "Come on lads, think of all the good performances we had up there in the Premier Division and take that into these games,"' recalls Nicholl. "You know how hard you had to work to draw at Ibrox and get those results, so if you work just as hard at this level against this opposition then you will get the game won quickly." It was really difficult. There was no consistency of results and poor performances. I just think it was an after-effect of missing the big games, the big stadiums, the big crowds and the attention from the press and all that.'

The squad had been unsettled over the summer as their manager was approached twice by Kilmarnock who wanted Nicholl as a replacement for Tommy Burns, who had left to manage Celtic.

'They came in and said they were going to treble my wages, it was as simple as that,' says Nicholl. The Rovers board knocked back the bids and the manager remained at Stark's Park.

'I don't wake up every morning and wish my life away about what might or might not have been,' Nicholl had said at the time. 'There have been two or three opportunities that for the right or wrong reasons didn't happen. I have a job to do as manager of Raith Rovers and I get on with it.'

Defender Shaun Dennis had also considered his own future over the summer. Speaking in the first few months of the season, he outlined his thinking. 'I initially refused to re-sign at the end of last season because I hoped I might get a move,' he said, 'but no one came in for me and I thought my weight might be putting them off. So I decided to do something about it.

'I cut out all the junk food I used to eat and I've lost half a stone so far. I had a long talk with Jimmy during the summer and we agreed that the best way for me to get on was to sign a one-year deal. I've been told that I can go if anyone comes in with the right money.'

Gordon Dalziel was once again contemplating life away from Stark's Park. 'I had a feeling it was time to move on,' says Dalziel. 'I'd only started 20 games in the Premier League although I still managed eight goals.'

A frank exchange with Nicholl after a close-season training session persuaded the striker to commit his future to the Kirkcaldy club. Nicholl would later hand Dalziel the captaincy of the club, a move that delighted the veteran.

'It was great of Jimmy Nicholl to give me the captaincy that year,' he says. 'I did have a laugh with my team-mates but when it came down to business, I was a serious person and the guys that played alongside me knew that and I think Nicholl saw that.'

The vote of confidence from the manager was a special moment. 'All the great experiences I had at the club, I would probably give them up for that moment. Here was a manager who I never thought I would see two weeks with, saying, "You're the captain of the club." It was probably one of the highlights of my career.'

Among the rest of the squad there was still a belief that they could challenge for promotion. 'It wasn't nice being relegated,' says Davie Sinclair. 'We were gutted, but we still had a good squad and we thought if we keep everybody together here we have a chance of going straight back up, but we knew it was going to be tough.'

Colin Cameron was quietly confident. 'We had pretty much the same group of players as the last season, who had got us promoted the season before that in the division,' he says. 'We were a year more experienced, especially the younger ones, and we had improved as a team. No one was feeling sorry for themselves because we had been relegated. I think there was just an added determination to get back into the Premier League at the first time of asking.'

Early results in the league disappointed, with four draws and a defeat to local rivals Dunfermline.

'I decided to stick by the same players despite our relegation, but even in the First Division we were absolutely hopeless in those early months,' says Nicholl. 'We were all on a bit of a downer. I was beginning to have doubts over a few of my players. We certainly didn't look like a team who were capable of pushing for promotion.'

'When you get relegated, everybody wants to get at you, so it took us at least the first quarter of games to find our feet,' says

Stevie Crawford. 'It was like you are the big fish in that division for that year and everyone wants a crack at you.'

It was to be the League Cup that offered respite from the poor league form. 'We couldn't really put our finger on it at the time, but it was like all of a sudden it is a cup game and you can relax,' recalls Davie Sinclair. 'The league games were totally different as there seemed to be more at stake.'

Kilmarnock arrived at Stark's Park on 31 August for the third round of the League Cup. An impressive crowd of 4,181 turned up to witness a thrilling match. There was a new face in the Rovers starting line-up with former Dundee United defender David Narey making his debut.

Narey was an imposing centre-back who had spent 21 years at United, much of it under the management of Jim McLean. Throughout his career, Narey's talent attracted the interest of many clubs but he was content to remain in Dundee.

'I was kept informed of moves which were made for me over the years,' he says. 'I remember being told that Southampton were interested, and also Leeds United while Jock Stein was there, but I never went knocking on the manager's door wanting to find out if clubs were making enquiries.

'I suppose the fact that I had never lived anywhere but Dundee helped United hold on to me. I didn't push for a transfer because I wasn't sure if I would settle elsewhere. The money might have been better but I wonder if I would have had the same peace of mind.'

His decision to stay at Tannadice was made easier by the success the Tayside club experienced in that period. He won the Scottish League Cup in 1979 and 1980, and the Scottish Premier League title in 1983. He played on some memorable European nights and captained the team in the 1987 UEFA Cup Final.

He represented Scotland 35 times and, like Nicholl, featured at the 1982 and 1986 World Cups, memorably opening the scoring for Scotland against Brazil in 1982 with his famous 'toepoke'.

His post-match comment on the goal was typically modest. 'I was lucky enough to catch the ball properly with my right foot and it went in,' he said.

His self-effacing nature was reinforced when he was awarded an MBE in 1992 for services to football. Reports suggested that the gist of his response to the award was, 'I'm only a footballer.'

His Dundee United career came to an end on 20 May 1994, the day before the team played Rangers in the Scottish Cup Final, a game that the Tannadice club would win with a goal from ex-Rover Craig Brewster. Although he had just been released, Narey celebrated jubilantly at the end of the match with no hint of bitterness or envy, despite having previously lost four Scottish Cup finals with the Tayside club. Nicholl persuaded the 38-year-old to sign on at Raith Rovers until the end of the following season.

Around the same time, Nicholl added another veteran player to the squad in Ian Redford. The midfielder from Perth had also starred for Dundee United during their successful European years, playing in the club's famous win over Barcelona in the Nou Camp and memorably scoring the winning goal for the Tannadice club against Borussia Moenchengladbach in the semi-final of the UEFA Cup in 1987.

Redford had started his career in 1976 across the street at Dens Park where he quickly became a star by scoring 34 goals in 85 games for Dundee. He attracted attention from a number of English clubs but signed for Rangers for £210,000, making him Scottish football's most expensive signing at the time.

The move placed a considerable amount of pressure on the young midfielder. 'I feel I lost some confidence when I moved to Rangers,' says Redford. 'Initially, I found it quite overwhelming being the most expensive player in Scotland. There are certain clubs which bring unique pressures for players and Rangers is one of them.'

He won four domestic cups with the Ibrox side between 1980 and 1985 before joining Dundee United. After leaving Tannadice, Redford went on to play for Ipswich Town, St Johnstone and Brechin. He had just resigned from his position as manager of Brechin City when Nicholl offered him the chance to play again in Kirkcaldy.

'Luckily for me, literally within days of my leaving Brechin City, I got a call from Raith Rovers manager Jimmy Nicholl, an old team-mate at Rangers,' he recalled. 'He offered me a cameo role for the rest of the season and also signed up Dundee United legend Davie Narey. Davie and I played together for three seasons at Dundee United and I knew him really well.'

Narey and Redford took their places in the Rovers starting 11 for the Kilmarnock game. The match kicked off and after 33 minutes the Ayrshire side took the lead through Ray Montgomerie. Rovers didn't panic and within two minutes were back level when Colin Cameron equalised.

Six minutes later, Rovers went in front when a Julian Broddle cross was headed back across the face of goal by Ally Graham to be met by Colin Cameron, who despite having his back to the goal, hit a fantastic overhead bicycle kick into the net. The *Scotsman* would later describe it as 'a goal German World Cup star Jurgen Klinsmann would have been proud of'.

Rovers retained their lead until half-time and knew they were just 45 minutes away from a place in the quarter-finals.

In the second half Kilmarnock pushed hard for an equaliser, with striker Bobby Williamson thrown on in an attempt to save the game, but Rovers entered the last 15 minutes still a goal ahead.

The pressure was eased with 13 minutes to go when Cameron completed his hat-trick, combining once more with Graham to undo the Kilmarnock defence. Any relief was short-lived as just two minutes later substitute Williamson pulled a goal back to set up a tense final ten minutes. Kilmarnock threw everything at Rovers but the Kirkcaldy club held out to secure a deserved 3-2 win. It had been a terrifically entertaining and emotionally draining cup tie.

After the match Cameron commented, 'That was the hardest 90 minutes for a long time but it is great to be in the quarter-final.'

What the young midfielder didn't tell the assembled reporters was that his pre-match preparation had consisted of a visit to McDonald's.

'It wasn't until a few weeks after that Colin told us that he had gone to McDonald's for his pre-match,' laughs Stevie Crawford. 'If Jimmy Nic had found out he would have killed him but after his hat-trick he would have probably tried to get him a loyalty card.'

Cameron reluctantly admits to his unorthodox match preparation. 'It was true. I don't even know why I did it. I tried it after that game once and funnily enough it didn't work, so I don't think it had any bearing on what I did in the game,' he laughs.

It was only the second hat-trick of his career, the other having been scored over in Ireland when playing for Sligo Rovers. He was delighted when journalists told him that he would receive £500 for posting a hat-trick. In the end, the cash never materialised and instead he was given the slightly disappointing consolation of a Coca-Cola watch from the cup sponsors.

Nicholl was delighted to be in the next round. 'Any sort of success gives players a boost and keeps them on their toes,' he says. 'In fact everyone associated with the club gets a lift. It's certainly a buzz for me and beating Kilmarnock caused a fair bit of excitement around the town.'

That night would produce another significant League Cup result as Falkirk knocked out Rangers in Glasgow. Ex-Rover John McStay was a substitute for Falkirk at Ibrox but his thoughts remained in Kirkcaldy.

'I was on the bench of the Falkirk team that beat Rangers at Ibrox in the Coca-Cola Cup,' says McStay. 'The first thing I did that night was jump in the car and travel up to Kirkcaldy because Rovers had beaten Kilmarnock. I still wanted to be up there, so I drove up and we went to Jackie O's with all my pals at Raith Rovers.'

With one half of the Old Firm knocked out, the potential opponents for the quarter-final started to look slightly less ominous. When Rovers were handed an away tie to fellow First Division team St Johnstone in the next round, the fans started to believe that they could progress to their first major semi-final since 1963.

11

EXPECTATIONS
Perth, September 1994

DANNY LENNON picked up the ball deep inside his own half. He controlled it and set off towards the St Johnstone goal. There were just seven minutes left of the quarter-final tie. Rovers led 2-1 but had been under intense pressure from the Perth team so Lennon's thoughts were as much on giving his team-mates a few seconds' respite.

With a Saints defender rapidly approaching, he poked the ball through to Colin Cameron on the left near the halfway line and continued his run. Cameron controlled the ball, checked and fed a perfect pass back to Lennon. The St Johnstone defenders had tried to play him offside but Paul Cherry in the centre was just too slow in stepping up and left Lennon with a clear route to goal. The only problem was he still had half the length of the pitch to travel and as he scampered forward, it seemed to take an age.

When he finally reached the box, Saints goalkeeper Andy Rhodes dived to block his run, but Lennon stabbed the ball past him and into the net. The 2,000 Rovers supporters packed in the stand behind the goal erupted as Lennon ran to accept their acclaim. Rovers were as good as in the League Cup semi-final and their fans knew it.

It had been a thrilling quarter-final, in front of 6,287 spectators, with Rovers dominating the game from early on. In the 20th minute Rovers took the lead through the unlikely source of Shaun Dennis. The big defender had been drafted into the team as a replacement for the injured David Narey.

'The lads had told me the bookies had me at 33-1 to score the first goal,' recalls Dennis. 'I thought about having a few bob on myself but decided my money was safer in my pocket with my scoring record. None of my team-mates bothered to bet on me either.'

Ten minutes later, Rovers edged further ahead when a counter-attack ended with Ally Graham sweeping the ball into the net. It was the striker's fifth goal of the season, but the only one he hadn't scored with his head. Rovers reached half-time with a two-goal advantage and were looking comfortable.

The second half was a tense affair after Paul Sturrock's team pulled a goal back on 50 minutes through John O'Neill. Saints then battered Rovers, hitting the woodwork twice. Graham had a golden chance to finish the tie when Stevie Crawford's perfect ball left him the simple task of directing his header towards an empty goal from three yards out. His header flashed wide and he sunk his face into the turf in embarrassment.

St Johnstone pushed hard for the equaliser until Lennon broke away, scored and put the game beyond doubt.

Cameron recalls the relief the team felt when Lennon managed to score. 'It was close and near the end we were like, "You know what if they get an equaliser, then it is going to be really tough for us to get back in the game, even though it would only be 2-2",' he says. 'It was just a relief that the third goal went in. Then after the game it was, "Jesus, we're in the semi-final." It was a great achievement.'

The *Daily Record* later commented that at the final whistle the Raith fans celebrated as if they had won the trophy itself. They were entitled to enjoy the moment as it was the club's first semi-final in 31 years.

Goalscorer Lennon was just happy to have secured the win for his manager. 'Jimmy has helped to revive my career and I have a lot to thank him for,' he told reporters after the match. 'Hopefully that goal will go some way to repay his faith in me.

'I'd been at Hibs since I left school. Maybe I was going stale. It ended up that I would have moved anywhere just to be with a side who wanted me in their first team. I knew Raith were going down, but Jimmy Nicholl sounded so ambitious that I jumped at the chance and it has given me a new lease of life.'

The following day, Lennon represented the Kirkcaldy side at the semi-final draw with Rovers, Aberdeen, Celtic and Airdrie left in the competition. Lennon was in no doubt about which team he wanted and, like most of the supporters, he was delighted when the draw paired Rovers with Airdrie. It gave both teams a terrific chance to progress to the final.

'We definitely fancied our chances,' recalls Scott Thomson. 'We were well used to playing them and it was a game that was winnable and they probably thought the same.'

Lennon could not hide his delight when he spoke to the gathered media after the draw. 'I'm delighted we've drawn Airdrie,' he said. 'It's given us a great chance of going all the way. I'm sure Airdrie will be looking at it the same as us.' He concluded with a smile, 'Anything is possible for Raith Rovers.'

The favourable draw started to make some of the players think about winning the cup for the first time.

'We were a tiny club from Kirkcaldy,' says Stephen McAnespie. 'We were just thinking about getting through each round and we were happy if we got our highlights on TV that night! You didn't want to look past the next game, but once you are in the semi-final you think, "We have a great shot at this if we take care of the semi-final."'

The match would be played at McDiarmid Park, an added bonus for the Rovers players after having just won at the same venue. There would be almost a month-long gap between quarter-final and semi-final and intriguingly they would have to play Airdrie twice, once in the league and once in the Challenge Cup.

The league match finished goalless and the Challenge Cup tie was also drawn, 1-1, after extra time. Cameron missed a spot-kick meaning that Airdrie progressed to the next round 5-3 on penalties.

'Big John Martin saved my penalty and we got knocked out,' recalls Cameron. 'It was weird because I remember saying right after missing my penalty, "If it goes to penalties in the semi-final, I am still taking one." I was so determined.'

If the players had not already been aware that the semi-final was going to be a keenly-contested, close match, they knew it after the two games against Airdrie.

Jimmy Nicholl decided to take the squad away in the build-up to the game. 'That was a bonus for the boys,' says McAnespie. 'We were, "They are taking us away somewhere. How good is that?" In this day and age that sort of thing is expected but back in those days for us to go to a hotel was, "Wow!" Jimmy, by all accounts, fought hard for that and it was a big deal.'

Nicholl chose the Nivingston House Hotel, a secluded mansion dating from 1725 near Loch Leven. There were rumours that the hotel was haunted and a listing on the Scottish Ghosts website describes an apparition of an 'old woman dressed in night clothes and the sound of heavy footsteps and doors closing when nobody is about' in a room in which a former owner shot himself in the early 1900s.

Nicholl recalls going to speak to the night porter about some unusual happenings in his room, 'I went down to see the porter and he told me I'd better sign the visitors' book and sure enough there were dozens of other supernatural sightings and bizarre happenings that had occurred within the hotel, noted in the book. "Has the ghost got into bed with you?" the porter asked. I read on and there was an old woman ghost who sneaked into people's beds and left a cold presence next to you.'

Some of his players later claimed that Nicholl decided to sleep with his suitcase next to him just in case.

For a Rovers squad renowned for wind-ups, it was too much temptation. 'A lot of the boys were hiding behind curtains and doors and then jumping out on people,' recalls Gordon Dalziel. 'Big David Sinclair was a big, tough central defender and there was one incident when some of the boys jumped out on him and he ran off as fast as anybody I have ever seen.'

Stevie Crawford laughs as he describes the incident, 'Me, Jason and Sinky went up to Jimmy's room and he gave us his car keys and said, "Go down to the petrol station and get the boys whatever they want: juice, sweets or whatever."

'Before we left he was telling us all about the ghost and the noises and that. We were walking down the corridor and started talking about what we would do if something jumped out on us.

So we are in our room just about to leave and there is a chap near the window and we all look at each other thinking, "No chance. This is a wind-up. Go and you have a look out the window. No you have a look."

'Sinky goes over and just before he is about to draw the curtains, Danny jumps out giving him the biggest fright in the world. The funniest thing about it was that Sinky ran away and later on they did it to young Brian Potter and he attacked Danny. Potts was also from High Valleyfield and seven years younger so you can imagine how much stick Sinky took for months afterwards with us saying, "We know who the real hard man of the Valleyfield boys is."'

At breakfast the next morning, Graham and Dalziel recounted tales of seeing a shadowy figure at the bottom of Dalziel's bed. Their team-mates weren't sure whether or not to believe them.

'I just remember laughing at Ally and Daz at breakfast the next morning,' says McAnespie. 'They swore to God they had seen something and the manager of the hotel came down and he confirmed the story, that what they had seen had been confirmed by other people. I don't know if they paid that manager to come and tell the story. I have no idea.

'We are still sceptical but the great thing about that was it took a lot of tension away from the preparation side. It broke the ice. Whether they contrived it or not, it didn't matter; it was something for the boys to laugh about when there was a lot of pressure.'

Thomson recalls that the squad was allowed out for a drink on the Saturday night, but with strict instructions to be back in the hotel just after midnight or they would be fined.

'Jimmy says, "Just go and chill out and have a few beers but I want you back in the hotel at half past 12," says Thomson. 'We all went into the pub in Kinross and at the end of the night we tried to get a taxi back. There were only about two taxis in Kinross and 20 of us trying to get back to the hotel.'

He describes the panic that ensued as the players tried to find a way back to the hotel in time to avoid a fine. 'The boys all just split up,' says Thomson. 'I ended up going up to this stranger's house and chapping on his door and said, "You wouldn't mind taking us back to the hotel, would you?"

'The boy says, "Aye, no bother." We were driving past everyone in the street and big Shaun Dennis was waving and trying to stop us but we kept going and got back in time. That was our preparation for the game.'

Wives, girlfriends and families were invited to the hotel for lunch on the Sunday afternoon and then the squad were left to focus on the semi-final. A number of players were struggling with injury. Nicholl had initially been hopeful of playing but decided he was too much of a risk and ruled himself out.

'I thought I had a wee chance after training on the Monday morning but felt the reaction and couldn't afford to take the risk,' he says. 'I needed my two substitutes badly and wasn't prepared to take the gamble on such an important occasion for the club.'

Striker Dalziel was also struggling but was such an important player in attack that Nicholl decided to risk him. 'I had a fitness test the day before and a fitness test at McDiarmid,' says Dalziel. 'It was a little bit sore but I didn't want to miss the semi-final. Nicholl said, "We can get an hour and if you have to come off, you have to come off."'

Julian Broddle was also struggling with injury but was so desperate to play in such an important game for the club that he hid the fact from his team-mates and manager.

'All the League Cup games I was injured but I didn't want to miss the chance of being in the final,' recalls Broddle. 'In the quarter-final and the semi-final I could hardly run. I don't know if Jimmy Nic was aware of it, I'm sure he was but I hid it because I knew if I lost my place I would struggle to get it back.

'I had a pulled muscle in my calf and hurt my groin as well and I remember thinking, "Oh my God, what am I doing?" But I was still getting through it and I never told the manager. I couldn't lose my spot. I would have been out of the team and history would have changed.'

The Rovers support was excited at the prospect of a semi-final and the club managed to sell most of their allocation for the stadium. Nicholl was in confident mood when he addressed the press for the final time.

'Airdrie will fancy themselves to have the edge because they've been through this situation so many times,' he said. 'However, I feel this occasion will bring out the best in my players. There are no negative thoughts among my players and we haven't even thought of the possibility of extra time and penalties. We've sold our 5,500 tickets and want to give our fans something in return.'

There was to be one final moment of farce in the build-up to the game as the team bus left Kinross without defender David Narey.

'I was a stickler for time and I didn't realise David had missed the bus,' says Nicholl. 'We were up at the ground and Martin Harvey says to me, "Davie Narey is not on the bus." He thought that I had given him permission just to take the car up because he was in Dundee. I said, "I never gave him permission. He should be on the bus." So I phoned the hotel and I never even had a chance to say what I was going to say. They said, "You're alright Jimmy, he's away."'

Once the hotel staff had realised that Narey had been left behind the chef had stepped in and was already driving him to the stadium.

As the players sat in the McDiarmid Park dressing room, preparing for the match, it began to sink in just how big a game it was.

'They even had these flashy programmes,' recalls Broddle. 'We never normally got posh, expensive programmes and everybody was trying to grab one in the changing rooms as a memento.'

The tension rose as kick-off approached. 'A lot of nerves started to kick in because a lot of us had never been to that level before,' recalls McAnespie. 'I think the older guys were a lot more nervous than the younger guys. We were just playing a game, but the older guys knew that this was their last hurrah and I think they were feeling that a little bit.'

As the teams emerged from the tunnel, the disparity in support was apparent. The stands to their left and straight ahead were packed with Rovers fans. In contrast, there were large empty spaces in the Airdrie end.

'I remember looking at the Airdrie support and thinking, "Airdrie should have a better support than that",' says Ally Graham. 'We had the other stands and it was almost full.'

The expectant Rovers support had turned out in numbers to roar their team to the League Cup Final. Now all the players had to do was win the game.

12

THE YOUNGEST WAS THE MOST LOVED
Perth, October 1994

B RIAN POTTER took his place in the dugout at
McDiarmid Park on the cold October evening in Perth.
He was just 17 years old, but as Ray Allan was cup-tied,
having played for Motherwell in an earlier round, Potter fulfilled
the role of substitute goalkeeper. Potter was a likeable and hard-
working Fifer who was trying to establish himself in the game.
He had decided early on in his football career that he would
concentrate on goalkeeping.

'I enjoyed playing outfield,' says Potter. 'But when I was ten or
11, I made my mind up that I wanted to concentrate on playing in
goals. Even at the high school, when I was 14 or 15, I still played
outfield now and again but I decided running about too much
wisnae for me!'

He had joined Raith Rovers as an apprentice as the club had
been promoted to the Premier Division. 'To know you were going
in full-time and it was Rovers' first year in the Premier League
was a big thing,' says Potter. 'All I wanted to do was to give it my
best shot. It helped there were quite a few local guys in the team. I
knew the likes of Davie Sinclair, Stevie Crawford and Jason Dair.
Then people like Daz, Peter Hetherston, Ronnie Coyle, big Ally

Graham and Tam Carson. They were good boys and they made you feel welcome.'

The introduction of the Premier Reserve League meant that the second-choice goalkeeper would often feature for the reserves on a Saturday, leaving Potter to act as substitute for the first team. It was a fantastic experience for someone starting out in the game.

'I remember my first game on the bench was at Tynecastle,' recalls Potter. 'Even going out for the warm-up and stuff with big crowds, I was a bag of nerves. Then I played up at Dundee United on the last day of the season when we were already relegated. We managed to win 3-2. Rovers had a good crowd up that day and it was a great experience.'

He continues, 'I had a great relationship with Scott [Thomson] and I still do. At the time we didn't even have a goalkeeping coach, so it was just me and Scott. We just worked away and trained together.'

Potter settled in to watch the semi-final. Jimmy Nicholl had selected a strong midfield of Lennon, Kirkwood, Sinclair and Cameron, supporting the two experienced strikers, Dalziel and Graham. The defence was developing a consistent look with Dennis and Narey flanked by McAnespie and Broddle.

David Narey had proved to be a steady influence since his arrival. Defensive partner Shaun Dennis spoke of his impact in the run-up to the game.

'He is a quiet man off the park but on the park he shows a split personality,' said Dennis. 'He talks away all the time and does his fair share of bawling. He is always telling us what to do and where we should be.'

Ally Graham joked that Narey was so quiet off the park it was hard to determine the big defender's personality.

'Don't ask me what big Dave is like,' said Graham. 'I haven't yet heard him speak. He simply comes into the ground in the morning, does his bit, and then goes away again. Mind you, his experience shines through on the park for us and he has been a terrific help for our younger players.'

Stevie Crawford laughs at what the experienced Narey must have thought of the younger players in the Rovers dressing room at the time.

'See when I think about Davie Narey coming in and sitting watching what Sinky, Barry Wilson, myself and Jason were doing. He must have been sitting there thinking, "Is there any chance of you lot growing up?" He just had a wry smile on his face all the time.' The referee blew his whistle and Dalziel rolled the ball to Graham. The 1994 League Cup semi-final was under way. The opening moments of the game were tense as both sides tried to come to terms with the sense of occasion.

Rovers appeared nervous at first, but settled quickly and were soon starting to create the better chances. Julian Broddle floated in a cross from a free kick which found Colin Cameron on the far right. He directed the ball back across the box, on to the head of Dalziel, who flashed the header wide. It had only been a half chance but it signalled Rovers' intent.

Minutes later, Graham was brought down clumsily and Steven McAnespie's shot from the free kick was accurate but lacked power, allowing John Martin to gather. Airdrie were finding it hard to contain the combination of Cameron's mobility and Graham's aerial power and were soon on the back foot again as Martin hesitated at a back-pass. His rushed clearance fell to Cameron, who blazed it high over the bar. It seemed only a matter of time before Rovers opened the scoring and just six minutes before half-time they duly did.

Cameron fed Narey in midfield and the experienced defender played the ball forward and uncharacteristically continued his run. The ball bounced off an Airdrie leg and found its way back to Narey on the edge of the box. His shot at goal was never going to trouble Martin and was easily blocked by a defender but instead of thumping the ball clear, the Airdrie defence tried to play their way out of trouble. Narey intercepted; the ball fell to Dalziel, who immediately squared it to Graham for the big striker to smash home a low shot from eight yards.

'I think big Narey had a nosebleed when he burst forward,' laughs Graham. 'The ball broke to Gordon Dalziel. I shouted to him to play it across and first-timed it with my left foot. I had to hit the perfect spot because if it had gone anywhere else the keeper would have saved it. That was definitely the most important goal of my career. It was a fantastic experience scoring in a semi-final.'

Rovers held their lead until half-time and returned to the dressing room in confident mood. At the start of the second half, Airdrie pushed for an equaliser but the Kirkcaldy side held firm. 'I can't remember jumping out of the dugout or getting upset about too many things,' says Nicholl. 'Things were going along nicely. We were feeling that this was going our way.'

As the time on the giant scoreboard inside McDiarmid Park approached 70 minutes, events took a dramatic turn. Jimmy Boyle launched a long, speculative ball forward, in search of Alan Lawrence. The pass was overhit but as Scott Thomson came for a routine catch, he strayed just outside his box. Quickly realising, he took a step backwards and caught the ball.

The Airdrie players and supporters reacted immediately and claimed that Thomson had handled the ball outside the area. Referee Bill Crombie glanced across to his linesman George Simpson, who had raised his flag to indicate that, in his opinion, Thomson had been over the line. Thomson protested his innocence but the referee awarded the free kick to Airdrie.

Thomson's sense of injustice increased as Crombie reached to his pocket and brandished a red card. The goalkeeper was stunned at the harshness of the decision and remains adamant that he was on the line when he gathered.

'I thought I was right on the line when I caught the ball,' says Thomson. 'I had plenty of time and I took a step back to get inside the area before catching the ball. I looked down and I was right on the line. The television replays have since shown I did gather the ball inside the box and to be fair to Bill Crombie, the next time he officiated one of our games he came up and said he shouldn't have sent me off. That was decent because he didn't need to say anything.'

Graham agrees that the ordering-off was harsh. 'I thought we were in control and if Scott hadn't been sent off we would have been comfortable winners,' says the striker. 'You look back now and see the sending-off and it was a bit ridiculous, wasn't it? A straight red card for that?'

It was Thomson's first career dismissal and as he left the pitch the enormity of what had just happened began to sink in.

'When I was walking off I was in a bad, bad place,' he says. 'I just didn't want to be there. I thought I had let everybody down;

the game was over. I got back in the dressing room and Jimmy had taken Davie Kirkwood off, so the two of us are sitting in the dressing room and I couldn't even speak to him. I was just devastated.'

On the Rovers bench the backroom team were involved in frantic preparations to get Thomson's replacement ready. Potter was hugely inexperienced but Nicholl had no option but to throw him on and hope for the best.

'Whether he was ready for it or not, we didn't know,' says Nicholl. 'It was a massive thing to go in to and you don't know how he is going to handle it. You are just hoping he gets through the game.'

Potter had no time to contemplate what he was about to face. 'I remember sitting in the back of the dugout and it is not a great view,' says Potter. 'I looked over to the linesman and I saw him flagging and I knew right away he was going to send him off, so I was starting to get stripped even before the red card was shown. I just saw the card going up and I thought, "Right, this is it." The manager just turned and said, "Get your top off. You're on."

'I had been on the bench for a year and never even had a chance of going on. You don't really expect it and for it to happen in the biggest game the club had had for years was a bit of a frightening experience.'

Around the Rovers team there was concern. Not only were they down to ten men for the rest of the match, they now had a young, inexperienced goalkeeper between the posts.

'Technically we trusted him, and in terms of shot stopping there were no questions about his ability,' says Stevie Crawford. 'He was a great lad but the one thing that always kept cropping up with Brian was his height. Would he be able to cope with an aerial bombardment? Anything on top of him you always felt it was going to be a battle for him.'

The Raith defenders realised they had to take on the additional responsibility of protecting Potter. Team-mate Davie Sinclair tried to reassure the young goalkeeper. 'He was nervous,' says Sinclair. 'We just said to him, "Look, just take your time. If it is coming across, shout for it and we will get out of your road. Talk to us, keep talking to us."'

Potter's immediate priority was to cope with the free kick that Thomson had just conceded. He lined up a wall of eight Rovers players in an attempt to keep Airdrie out.

'I think it was the biggest wall that has ever been built in football!' laughs Potter. 'The Airdrie fans were right behind me and they were letting me know what they thought about me: my height, my weight and my size and everything like that.'

The wall did its job as Kenny Black's powerful drive deflected off Graham's foot and flew inches wide of the goal.

Any thoughts Rovers had of holding on to their slender lead were extinguished just five minutes later. A neat passing move ended with Stevie Copper receiving the ball 20 yards out. He let the ball bounce twice and then hit it perfectly into the corner of the goal.

It was a terrific strike that few, if any, goalkeepers could have saved but Potter picked the ball out of the net and threw it away in frustration. 'I thought that was it, I'd let everyone down,' he says.

From that moment on, the target was to reach full time without conceding again. Rovers mounted what Hugh Keevins would later describe as 'an outrageous rearguard action' to stay in the tie.

'We knew we were up against it,' says Nicholl. 'There was no point of coming off cavalier and saying, "We still had a go at them" but then getting nothing out of it. It doesn't make me proud in a footballing sense to admit that I put Ally Graham back at centre-half, but some things you've got to do.'

It was a move appreciated by his young goalkeeper. 'Davie Narey and big Ally were just class,' says Potter. 'They were coming back for things and heading stuff away, because I wasn't the tallest. So I mostly had to pick up wee bits and pieces. Sinky was also immense and put a real shift in. If I had a pass back or a kick out he was always there to encourage me. They never really had that many opportunities to score.'

The team performed heroically in protecting Potter for the remainder of the match and when the referee blew his whistle to signal the end of the 90 minutes, the relief among the Rovers players was palpable.

'We had to roll our sleeves back up and show a lot of team spirit,' says McAnespie. 'We showed a lot of mettle and we showed we could dig deep. We could have got overwhelmed so easily and gone under. It took a big collective effort.'

Throughout extra time there was just one thought in most Rovers players' minds – get to penalties.

Potter was confident he could win the tie for his club in a shoot-out. 'Every time I had been in a penalty shoot-out, I had always saved at least one,' he says. 'I wanted it to go to penalties. I was never nervous at penalties because even way back to my time with different boys' clubs I had never lost a shoot-out and I'd been through five or six.'

Rovers successfully restricted Airdrie's chances and survived extra time. They were still in the tie and still had a chance of progressing to the final, although they knew that the shoot-out would test their mental strength and resilience even further.

Nicholl immediately started the search for volunteers to take the five penalties. 'I think a lot of the guys were looking to the ground and kidding on they had cramp,' jokes Graham, but the Rovers manager found his men – Shaun Dennis, Stevie Crawford, Danny Lennon, Steven McAnespie and Colin Cameron.

As Potter tried to prepare himself for his own role, Sinclair offered words of encouragement. 'I said to him, "Look, we're not going to tell you what to do, just make up your own mind",' says Sinclair.

'He was like, "Aye, aye. I'm fucking shitting myself." I said, "You're fucking shitting yourself? I'm fucking shitting myself too!"'

Rovers won the toss of the coin and elected to go first, with the penalties to be taken in front of the Airdrie supporters in the South Stand.

Dennis was first up and as he made the long walk from the halfway line for the first penalty he was watched by Rovers legend Andy Young. Young had played for the club a remarkable 611 times and had featured in their last appearance in the League Cup Final when they lost to Rangers in 1949.

Young had brought along his runners-up medal from that final and as Dennis advanced, Young placed his hand on the medal in his pocket. His hand remained there for every one of Rovers' spot-kicks.

Dennis placed the ball, took a long run-up and sent John Martin the wrong way to give Rovers a 1-0 lead. His composure was matched by Airdrie's Jimmy Boyle, who blasted the ball confidently down the middle to make it 1-1. McAnespie and Andy Smith then both scored with ease to keep the score tied at 2-2.

Cameron was third for Rovers and looked nervous as he walked forward. The midfielder had missed a penalty in the Challenge Cup tie between the sides a few weeks earlier.

'In the first game I changed my mind on the run-up and the keeper saved it well,' says Cameron. 'It was just a case of don't change your mind, simple as that. I just thought, "This is where I am putting it and if I hit it right, even if he guesses correctly, he is not saving it."'

Cameron sent Martin the wrong way to make it 3-2 to Rovers. The pressure was growing as each penalty was scored, with no one wanting to be the first to make a mistake. On the sidelines, both Dalziel and Broddle retreated to the tunnel to wait nervously for the conclusion. Potter remained confident as Paul Jack approached to take Airdrie's third penalty.

'I was just guessing which way to go,' he says. 'Our assistant manager, Martin Harvey, told me not to get beat standing up, just to go to one side and make myself as big as possible.'

He guessed right with Jack's penalty but the ball evaded him and landed in the right-hand corner. Jack broke into a broad smile as he returned to the centre circle having brought the score level again at 3-3.

Crawford was also mindful of Martin Harvey's advice as he arrived to take Rovers' next penalty.

'For some reason I always wanted the fourth penalty,' says Crawford. 'I think maybe it was the fact that by the fifth one it could be over and done with. Martin Harvey just said, "Hit the target. If you hit the target the keeper has got to make a save."'

Crawford scored to make it 4-3 to Rovers as Martin dived the wrong way for the fourth time. 'It was good advice,' smiles Crawford.

Kenny Black confidently levelled the score at 4-4. Potter again guessed right, but the shot had too much power and crossed the line. The first eight penalties had been expertly taken and there was no room for error as Danny Lennon strode forward to take Rovers' final kick.

The supporters from Kirkcaldy waited anxiously in the stands, knowing that a mistake now could prove fatal to their ambitions. Lennon fired the ball to the left and although John Martin guessed correctly for the first time, he lost his footing at the vital moment and Lennon's shot ended up just out of reach. Rovers led 5-4 and Alan Lawrence needed to score to keep the Lanarkshire side in the cup.

Lawrence walked slowly towards the goal. He knew he couldn't afford to fail but as the experienced striker was used to taking penalties he seemed a confident choice. As he approached the spot, Potter threw the ball high in the air. Lawrence had to check his walk and step back to catch the ball. It was a tactic that Potter hoped might break Lawrence's concentration.

'The ball was just in front of me and I saw he had quite a long walk,' says Potter. 'So I just decided to throw it up as high as I could. Hopefully that just delayed his reaction two or three seconds and put him off a wee bit.'

The young goalkeeper steadied himself on his line. 'I just stepped to my left, then dived to my right,' he recalls. 'I had an incline to go to my right. It was just a wee guess and obviously everything after that was a bit of a blur.'

Lawrence struck the ball in the direction of the goalkeeper and Potter saved it. An incredible roar went up from the far end of the ground from the Rovers support. Raith Rovers were in the final.

The young goalkeeper stood arms aloft in triumph as his team-mates sprinted to congratulate him. 'It was just the noise, two or three seconds of noise,' recalls Potter. 'After that I didn't have time to think what I'd done. The boys were right on top of me and the fans were on the park. It was unbelievable. They are the things you dream about; saving penalties and getting through to cup finals. What a buzz. What a thrill.'

From the two Raith Rovers stands, fans flooded on to the pitch in celebration. Lawrence had fallen to his knees in despair immediately.

'I had my head in my hands from the moment I saw the keeper save my penalty,' said Lawrence. 'I didn't have a clue what was going on. I didn't even know anyone else was on the park until Andy Smith told me to get to my feet. He told me I'd better get off because the Raith fans would end up jumping all over me if I didn't.'

The penalty save remains a moment that fans and players can recall with absolute clarity. 'You talk about good moments in your career,' says McAnespie. 'It will never get better than that. Potts made the save and the whole place went ballistic. I had never seen anything like it; the atmosphere and the adrenaline rush. It was amazing. It really was. We were off to a final.'

Potter was soon being carried off on the shoulders of fans. 'I remember trying to get to the tunnel and Martin Harvey came out of nowhere and was trying to pull me along and the fans were going daft,' says Potter. 'People were patting me on the head, slapping me on the back and trying to pick you up. It was just chaos. Your head is just a blur. You have just saved the penalty and the next minute you are on people's shoulders.'

Amid the chaotic scenes one man had more reason than most to thank Potter for his heroic performance.

'I can't thank Brian enough for what he did for the side and for me in particular,' says Scott Thomson. 'I thought I had blown it and all I could think was people would remember me as the man who cost us the semi-final. He pulled me out of a big hole. I just felt pure relief and joy.'

Thomson reflects on the extraordinary events of that night and believes that there was a degree of fate involved. 'I believe it was the way it was meant to be,' he says. 'If I had stayed on, maybe we wouldn't have won. It was to be Brian Potter's night. He was ready for it and he deserved all he got that night.'

It was only later that the young goalkeeper began to take in exactly what he had achieved. 'It wasn't until I was back in the changing rooms before I started to realise,' he says. 'All the players were just so happy that Raith Rovers were through to a major final. I got in to the dressing room and the boys were all jumping on top of me. It was total bedlam.'

The Rovers fans streamed out of the stadium in disbelief that their club had reached the final of a cup competition for the first time in decades. Most couldn't stop smiling as they headed back to their cars and buses and started the journey home down the M90.

They would soon be joined by the team bus which, according to Davie Sinclair, 'bounced' down the motorway.

On board was one man who had been associated with the club longer than most. Kitman John Valente had been a Raith Rovers supporter since the 1962/63 season. He owned a group of fish and chip shops in Kirkcaldy and had been a regular financial contributor to the club. He had joined the backroom staff under Frank Connor.

'Frank used to come up every Thursday for a fish supper and we always had a blether,' recalls Valente. 'He was one of these people that you just felt you had known him all your life. He said he had this youth team going off to France so I sponsored it for two years in a row. The second time Frank said to me, "Why don't you come along?"

'I went and spent time in the dressing room with Murray Cheyne, helping with the strips. Frank said, "Could you do this for the first team?"

'I said, "Aye, but I'll have to learn from the wife how to fold things!" So that is how I got involved. I would have done anything for the Rovers.'

It was a role he would perform expertly for 12 years. 'I only made one mistake,' says Valente. 'We were playing Hearts in the Premier and we had changed the sponsor to Kelly Copiers. I said to Jimmy, "We have the long-sleeve new strips but we don't have any of the short sleeves,' and he told me they were due in a couple of weeks. So I packed what I thought was the new strips. When I was putting them up at Tynecastle with the numbers facing me I thought, "Oh, we do have the short sleeves after all," but when they started to put them on to go out to train, I realised they were the old sponsors' shirts.

'I phoned the office at Stark's Park and the club photographer brought the strips across but it was so close to kick-off they wouldn't let him near the ground in his car. I got them at half-time, which was great but they played the first half with the old sponsor, John Grubb, and the second half with Kelly Copiers. I never got a row, but apparently Kelly phoned up on the Monday and he was raging.'

Valente would go on to become an integral part of the club. 'The work that John put in,' says Stevie Crawford. 'He used to come in with chocolate bars and Dairy Milks for the substitutes and all the players used to go up to his shop for fish suppers.'

The Raith players were delighted to see him celebrating the semi-final win. 'After the game I remember being on the bus with John Valente,' says Cameron. 'He never usually drank but he was on the bubbly and by the time we got back to Kirkcaldy he was absolutely bladdered. That sticks out because he loved the club, he loved being part of it all and he just let his emotions go because of what we had achieved. You saw how much it meant to him.'

Valente laughs as he recalls the events of that evening. 'I am not a drinker and had had nothing to eat all day,' he says. 'In the morning I had come up to the shop and had cups of coffee but no breakfast, no lunch, no tea and gone straight to the game. After we won they came in with this crate of champagne and the boys didn't want the champagne.

'They wanted the beer but I like anything sweet so there was me on the bus with this bottle of champagne. I couldn't even go to the party in the 200 Club when we got back, I was that drunk. My wife had to come down and pick me up.'

He would not be the only person missing out on some of the celebrations that night. Potter may have been the Rovers hero but he was not yet old enough to get into the local nightclub, Jackie O's, so as his team-mates continued their celebration he headed back home to celebrate with two meat pies and a cheese piece. It would be 4.30am before he finally fell asleep as he relived his moment of glory in his head over and over again.

The next morning Airdrie manager Alex MacDonald lamented his side's inability to get the better of ten men, but made a point of praising the achievement of the young goalkeeper. 'Good luck to the boy,' he said. 'I wish I was a teenager again and had just made a save which took my team through to a cup final.'

For the next few days, Potter was the centre of attention as every media outlet in Scotland appeared keen to speak to the young hero. 'We had all the papers in and even the local paper in Dunfermline wanted pictures,' Potter laughs. 'I took a fair bit of a ribbing from the ground staff for that.'

His team-mates were delighted that their hard-working friend was receiving the recognition he deserved. 'Potts will be always fondly remembered by the Raith fans, and rightly so,' says Jason Dair.

Julian Broddle believes Potter and the other young players were crucial in helping win the tie for Rovers. 'The young lads were the ones who carried us through that night,' he says. 'I don't think they were scared of losing. The older lads were thinking, "Maybe this is our last chance", but they didn't have that fear. They were all heroes. It was just amazing to think that we could get to a final, an incredible experience and incredible times.'

Raith Rovers had reached their first final in 45 years in the unlikeliest of circumstances. As they waited to see who their opponents would be, Nicholl considered the prospect. 'Now we can go to the final hoping that our opponents have an off-day, or are over-confident,' he said, adding with an air of disbelief, 'Who knows in this crazy game?'

Frank Connor in the Stark's Park dressing room

Celebrating promotion after a tense finish at Stair Park in 1987

Building a strong First Division squad

Jimmy Nicholl with chairman John Urquhart

The 'Policeman' in action

Gordon Dalziel leads the singing at the Christmas party

In the dugout

*Jock McStay and
John Valente
welcome the final
whistle to clinch
promotion*

*Craig
Brewster
and Ian
MacLeod
wind down*

Peter Hetherston in the directors' box

We are the Champions

The manager reflects on a magnificent achievement

Semi-final hero Brian Potter

The squad in their Coca-Cola Cup t-shirts

The teams emerge from the Ibrox tunnel

Stephen McAnespie tries to match Tom Boyd in the opening minutes

Stevie Crawford races towards the Govan Stand after opening the scoring

Gordon Dalziel equalises with minutes remaining

Unthinkable surely for the skipper to miss

The players enjoy their moment

PENS

RAITH		CELTIC	
DENNIS ✓	1-0	O'NEIL ✓	1-1
Dair ✓	2-1	Collins ✓	2-2
Cameron ✓	3-2	Walker ✓	3-3
Crawford ✓	4-3	Byrne ✓	4-4
McAnespie	5-4	Galloway ✓	5-5
Rowbotham ✓	6-5	McStay ✗	

A journalist's notepad records the penalty shoot-out

The team salute the Raith support in the Govan Stand

The whole club back at Jackie O's

Ronnie Coyle at his benefit match

Reunited for the Ronnie Coyle benefit match in 2011

13

AMBITIOUS OUTSIDERS
Kirkcaldy, October 1994

S TEPHEN McANESPIE awaited the result of the second semi-final between Aberdeen and Celtic to learn who Rovers would play in the final. The defender had a reason, more than most, to be interested in the outcome, having begun his career with the Pittodrie side.

'I started off at Aberdeen when I signed an S-form with Fergie,' says McAnespie. 'I was able to leave school at 15 to go professional so I signed an apprentice contract.' His time at Aberdeen was enjoyable but would come to an abrupt end when Willie Miller succeeded Alex Smith as manager.

'I didn't really see eye to eye with Willie Miller and when he got the job I was one of the first guys out the door,' he says. 'My contract was up and he didn't give me a new one, so I was on my bike.'

After being released by Aberdeen, McAnespie had a desire to play outside Scotland. He moved to Sweden and signed for Vasterhaninge IF, a club based near Stockholm.

'The Scandinavian thing was fashionable at the time,' he says. 'A lot of guys were taking a shot out there and there were a lot of Scandinavians coming this way. I had a good time there. I spent a season there and I loved it. It was brilliant but it was only going to be a short-term thing as I was too young at the time to lay down roots. If I had done it later in my career I would have stayed there forever.'

The young defender was considering his next move when a chance encounter between Jimmy Nicholl and his father raised the prospect of a contract in Kirkcaldy.

'I came back to Scotland with nothing in mind,' says McAnespie. 'I was looking to stay in Europe and my agent was looking at different places but my dad had been talking to Jimmy at a game and he was telling him that I was thinking of coming back. Jimmy said, "As soon as he gets back have him contact me."'

'I had another couple of options in Scotland but you looked at Jimmy and his pedigree and what he was trying to build in Kirkcaldy. As soon as I went in to speak to him there was no turning back. He could sell snow to the Eskimos.'

Nicholl's enthusiasm and honesty had impressed him. 'A lot of managers will blow smoke up your arse,' he says. 'They tell you all sorts of lies just to get you to sign but Jimmy was straight. He told you that you'd fight for everything you would get and you would battle but you would be given a genuine chance.'

McAnespie signed a short-term contract and was immediately impressed by the atmosphere at Stark's Park and the obvious quality in the Rovers squad.

'That short period gave me an opportunity to really see the quality of Crawford, Dair and Cameron,' he says. 'I could tell that we were really going to grow together as a team and I wanted to be part of that. So when we sat down at the end of the season it was a no-brainer. As soon as Jimmy asked me if I was interested in a long-term deal I said, "Yes, give me it." I didn't even ask him about money. I didn't care.'

The attraction of learning directly from Nicholl's considerable experience of playing at right-back appealed.

'I had a great opportunity to learn the game from him,' says McAnespie. 'As much as I had thought I had learned it, I was still a kid and having the opportunity to learn and define my game by playing and training with him was fantastic.'

McAnespie's signing coincided with the release of fellow right-back John McStay. 'I signed and then he released McStay,' he says. 'I think it was really a case of who put pen to paper first. I think it would have been different if I had sat back said, "Oh I don't know. Let's wait and see." McStay could maybe have signed and then I would have been the one on the outside.'

The decision to commit himself to Raith was one that McAnespie would not regret as just ten months later, he would be playing in a League Cup Final. Having found out that Celtic beat Aberdeen 1-0 at Ibrox to take their place in the final alongside Rovers, he now knew what lay ahead of him: Raith Rovers versus Celtic in the League Cup Final on 27 November 1994. Like most people associated with the Kirkcaldy club, he couldn't wait.

The excitement began to build immediately. Rovers were in a major final and would face one half of the Old Firm. As Hampden was being redeveloped, the final would be played at Ibrox Stadium.

There was initial disappointment among some of the squad and supporters that the final wasn't at the national stadium but it was soon forgotten as the reality of what lay ahead sank in. Nicholl commented, 'For the chance of being in a cup final I'd play it in the backyard.'

Fans started to clamour for tickets and organise their transport to the game. Jim Foy of the supporters' club recalls the madness of the weeks before the game. 'People were calling at all times of the day to book seats on the buses travelling to Ibrox,' he says. 'From the moment I got up in the morning until the time I retired for the night, the phone just kept on ringing.

'I get more satisfaction looking back to that period than any other time running the buses for the supporters' club. For all the work that was involved, and all the time that it took up, I like to think that I did my wee bit to help Rovers fans to be part of the biggest day in the history of Raith Rovers Football Club.'

As the final approached, the club had sold an astonishing 10,500 tickets. Despite the incredible achievement of selling the whole of the Govan Stand, it would mean that on the day of the final the Rovers support would still be outnumbered three to one by Celtic fans, who had been allocated the remaining three stands at Ibrox.

The disparity in support would not be the only difference between the sides. Newspapers reported in the run up to the final that the Rovers squad had cost just £215,000, with Ally Graham and Davie Kirkwood accounting for the lion's share of that total, compared to the Celtic squad assembled at a cost of £5.17m. This was truly a David and Goliath final.

Despite the gulf in resources, the Rovers players refused to be overawed. 'As soon as we were through, I knew there was no point in fearing Celtic,' says Colin Cameron. 'We had played some good teams to get through and we were not just going there to make up the numbers.'

The route to the final had helped develop a confidence in the squad that they could overcome any challenge, even a final against Celtic.

'Every round we played seemed to be a battle and that gave us extra belief,' says Stephen McAnespie. 'We overcame hurdles along the way, having to go to penalties and losing Scott in the semi-final, but we still managed to win. We started to believe that we could do something.'

Nicholl worked relentlessly to reinforce that belief into his players in the weeks leading up to the final. 'I knew over 90 or 120 minutes we could compete with the Old Firm,' says Nicholl. 'Anybody that plays against Celtic or Rangers knows you won't win the league over 38 games but over one game you have a chance. I had belief in my players and I knew if they went out there and were brave and got on the ball, then they could win the cup.'

The Kirkcaldy club received a major blow when club captain Danny Lennon suffered a broken metatarsal in a training accident. It was an injury that was to rule him out of the final.

'We were training,' says Lennon. 'One of the youngsters, Mark Quinn, who I used to pick up on the way through to the ground, mistimed a challenge and caught me. When I got up at first my foot just felt numb but once I tried to run, I heard it crack and it collapsed. I went for an x-ray and had it confirmed I had broken my metatarsal. There were a few tears but I knew I just had to get on with it.'

The loss of their influential skipper was a severe blow and there was an initial mood of despondency in the Rovers camp. 'Our physio Gerry Docherty told me all the boys were so depressed at the ground, it was as if someone had died,' says Lennon.

Slowly, the jokes and jibes returned. 'I was quite relieved when the lads started giving me stick instead of sympathy,' says Lennon. 'It started when I had my picture in the paper. Big Shaun came up and told me that the lads had seen the photos and decided that all the final bonuses would be going to me – on condition I used it to buy a new suite for my house. It raised my spirits.'

There was also personal tragedy for Julian Broddle in the build-up to the match, when his mother passed away.

'It was a difficult time for me,' recalls Broddle. 'I dashed down to the hospital in England just before my mum died. Then with the funeral and everything else, it was very hard. Then I was back up again to try and get into the right frame of mind for the cup final. It was a difficult time but the build-up just focused your mind and it pushed me on and I thought, "Well this is the time when we can hopefully do her proud and win the trophy."'

The preparation continued with Nicholl trying to maintain a sense of normality. It would prove challenging with the media demands of being in a cup final. There were constant press engagements, photocalls and other demands on his players.

He constantly talked down expectations in a bid to maintain Celtic's position as favourites for the tie. 'The only way I want to go into the final is as massive underdogs,' he said. 'I can't stop my players reading papers suggesting they have a chance of winning but I always found my best times came when I was the underdog.'

The manager's approach was soon being echoed by his players. When McAnespie was asked about his club's good form, he stressed that the Glasgow side were still overwhelming favourites, saying, 'Our recent league form has been good and hopefully we can carry that into Sunday's game. It's daft however to think that, just because Celtic's recent form has been poor, they won't be hot favourites for the final.'

McAnespie admits that it was part of a deliberate strategy to lower expectations.

'It was part of the club's thinking to play it down and it became part of the players' thinking,' he says. 'It came from Jimmy, his attitude in the press when he was talking to the media and how he approached things. It became how we all approached it. Anytime it was broached in the changing room or in team meetings it was always played down. It became the mantra.

'You didn't want to build something up then get disappointed. It would have disappointed us as players. It would have disappointed the people around the town. You don't want to be telling people something is going to happen and then it doesn't materialise.' The strategy worked in lowering expectation and removing much of the pressure from the Rovers squad in the build-up to the final.

Nicholl had initially told the team to put the cup final out of their minds and stressed that regaining their place in the Premier Division was more important. It was a message that the players attempted to take on board but most would find it difficult to ignore the looming cup final.

'It was always there,' says Cameron. 'You couldn't just block it out because of who it was against and it being a cup final. It was impossible to do but I tried to use it in a positive way to make damn sure I was playing as well as I could, to make it impossible for Jimmy not to play me.'

Most of his team-mates did the same and the form of the team going into the match was good. After a slight stutter against Dunfermline the weekend after the semi-final defeat of Airdrie, Rovers won all three of their games comfortably: 3-0 away against Hamilton, 4-2 at home against Stranraer, and a blistering 3-0 defeat of Clydebank the weekend before the final.

The performance against Clydebank injected a confidence into the team and was the moment when many of the players started to believe that they could win the cup.

'I remember when we went to Clydebank and got a 3-0 win,' says Ally Graham. 'I thought to myself, "By the way, we are a right good team." That is when everyone started to think, "We have a chance in this cup and we can play anybody and beat them." I just thought, "We are on a roll here and this is our cup. It has our name on it."'

Davie Sinclair served a one-match ban in the Clydebank game, meaning that he was free for selection for the final. He had endured a nervous few days as his team-mates taunted him about the prospect of the game being postponed, meaning he would be banned for the final.

'Ally turned up for training and told me Kilbowie was under a foot of water,' says Sinclair. 'When he saw the worry on my face he suggested I need to get down there with a hairdryer and a straw to try and dry the pitch out. I spent the rest of the week worrying that the game might be off.'

If Rovers were confident and scoring goals, at Celtic Park the opposite was true. Celtic's results approaching the final had been poor, with only one win in eight games. Their last two matches before the final had been mediocre goalless draws with Partick Thistle and Kilmarnock.

There was huge expectation among the Celtic supporters that after five years without success the team would finally end their trophy drought. If the Raith Rovers approach was to dampen expectation, the levels of expectation at Celtic seemed to increase daily as the final approached.

Manager Tommy Burns described it as a game that they could not afford to lose. 'This game and the chance it gives us is perhaps the most important that I can ever remember for Celtic,' said Burns. 'It is vital that we win.'

His captain, Paul McStay, continued the theme when he spoke of the intense pressure in the days before the final. 'Everywhere I go people come up and say to me, "We must win it" and I agree with them,' he said. 'I hate to think I'd look back one day and realise that I was the Celtic captain who won nothing.'

The journalists covering the preparations of both teams were acutely aware of the pressure on the Glasgow side. 'What I remember very much in the build-up was the intense pressure on Celtic,' says broadcaster Richard Gordon. 'They hadn't won anything in a while and Fergus McCann had come in and this match would almost be the redemption if you like.

'The club had been saved and this was going to be the day when they became winners again. There was clearly nervousness there.

'I remember going across to the Raith open day to interview the players and it was a complete contrast from the mood that was around Celtic at the time. Jimmy Nic was the life and soul of the party and there was almost a sense of wonderment that they had reached the final.

'They were full of life and enthusiasm and you never got the sense that they were overawed in any way. They were just going out to have a blast and enjoy themselves.'

In Kirkcaldy, the anticipation continued to build. 'The week leading up to it was incredible,' recalls Sinclair. 'The excitement in the town, getting interviewed every other day and we went into schools. It was brilliant.'

There was a reminder of Rovers' illustrious past when the club assembled Jockey Maule, Andy Young, Willie Penman, Harry Colville and Andy Leigh for the waiting media. The five had played in the club's last League Cup Final appearance in 1949 when Rovers had taken on Rangers at Hampden. The Kirkcaldy side had lost the final 2-0 but performed well and earned praise from the press.

Rovers' groundsman Andy Leigh recalled his experience of being selected for the final as a young boy and having to be walked along Argyle Street in Glasgow by his father to calm his nerves before the match.

He was confident that the current squad would not experience the same nerves, saying, 'It's a 50-50 chance if you get to the final. It doesn't matter who you are playing. It's only 90 minutes.'

It was a theme Nicholl reinforced to his players behind closed doors. 'Privately, I remember looking at Celtic's performances and saying to the players, "I know it is a different division but Celtic aren't playing well so you have a wee chance here,"' recalls Nicholl.

Publicly, Nicholl continued to stress that Rovers were the clear underdog. At his final press interviews he stated his concern about his squad freezing on the day.

'My worst fear is that they will collapse on the day,' he said. 'It's about the only thing about the build-up that gives me palpitations. I worry that the day might go totally wrong and we won't do ourselves justice. Celtic might get an early goal and go on to win four or five nothing and I would really hate to see that happen especially for the 11,000 fans we are taking with us.'

He outlined what he would be saying to his players in advance of the final. 'I am going to be sitting the boys down for a wee chat between now and Sunday and telling them to ask themselves a couple of questions,' he said. 'I want each player to ask himself, "Can I as an individual compete successfully with my opposite number for 90 minutes, and can we as a team match Celtic?" And if their answers, as I anticipate, are a resounding "Yes," then I'll tell them, "Let's go for it."'

He concluded his thoughts with a wry smile at the thought of his club in Europe. 'We're the biggest underdogs ever, but, yes we are a game away from Europe,' he said. 'For a club who were part-time in the Second Division not so long ago, wouldn't that mean something?

'I find the thought that we might be just 90 minutes from gaining entry into Europe laughable. No disrespect to this club, the area or its people, but it is hard to contemplate such a possibility. Imagine us being paired with AC Milan, them trying to look up a map of Scotland and find Raith and Fabio Capello calling us asking for training facilities in Burntisland. It is quite funny.'

The comments dominated the following day's headlines and had the helpful consequence, whether intentional or not, of diverting attention from his team and their readiness for the task ahead. For Nicholl, the attraction of European football was real.

'The motivation thing on my part was Europe,' he says. 'That was the only thing I ever spoke about. I said, "Listen lads, when are you ever going to have the chance to be in Europe again? It will never happen again. This is the last time you will get a chance to represent Raith Rovers in Europe. Win the cup, great, but look what it is leading to. You will be representing Raith Rovers in Europe."'

In his final comments to the press, captain Gordon Dalziel joked with reporters about the chances of him scoring a vital goal in the final. 'I have always been lucky in the sense that whenever I needed a goal I would get one, even if it went in off my backside. So it could happen again this weekend,' he said.

Rovers spent the remaining days before the final at a hotel in Erskine. The focus was on getting the squad prepared and trying to retain as much sense of normality as possible, given the circumstances. The squad trained at Dumbarton's Boghead ground on Friday morning and then attended the Rangers versus Aberdeen game at Ibrox on the Friday night.

On the Saturday, the players returned to Ibrox for another light training session. It was an opportunity only afforded the Kirkcaldy club because of Nicholl's contacts at Ibrox.

'I remember we sneaked into Ibrox because they had just laid the pitch,' says Dalziel. 'We sneaked in the back door at Ibrox and did a wee training session on the pitch prior to the final. I think Jimmy used his connections there.'

It would not be the only bit of assistance the club would get from their Ibrox hosts as on matchday a box of studs more suited to the Ibrox pitch was left in the Rovers dressing room. 'I remember the Rangers kitman saying to me, "Anything you want, just ask," says John Valente. 'He said, "If you want more balls or anything, just as long as you beat that shower."'

Nicholl had assessed his players during the two training sessions as he contemplated his starting 11 for the final. He had weighed up the attributes his side would need to compete against a strong Celtic team. His biggest challenge was how to cope with a midfield that included the quality and experience of John Collins and Paul McStay.

He had already ruled himself out of a starting position, saying, 'There will be enough pressure without me sucking air trying to get to grips with Celtic's midfield.'

The loss of Danny Lennon had left him with a difficult choice in the centre of the park. 'The biggest decision I had to make was whether to go with the young players or the senior players,' recalls the manager. 'You think, do you go with the senior players because they're experienced or let the young players go out and enjoy it and express themselves because they'll be full of running?'

He knew that whatever decision he made there would be somebody disappointed. 'Whatever way I went it wouldn't be nice for those left out, especially as I couldn't promise them another crack at it the next year,' says Nicholl. 'I didn't want to deprive any of the players of that opportunity. For many of my players, this final would be the biggest game of their football lives. How could I take that away from them?'

He knew that he couldn't hope to match the experience of Collins and McStay in midfield, so if his team were going to win, then they would have to do it with youth and energy. He decided to select Jason Dair, Colin Cameron and Stevie Crawford for his starting line-up. It was a bold decision that would surprise many.

'You just knew they were comfortable on the ball,' says Nicholl. 'You knew wee Mickey was going to be a threat with his runs. You knew Crawford and Dair had good ability. They had energy, were enthusiastic and just had everything going for them.

'I worried that it might be too much for them and there might have been certain times in the game where you need the experienced ones, but I thought, "Just let the kids go and run the legs off them." They were fearless and energetic.

'It wasn't just a case of throwing them in. They had jobs to do. "Go and take the ball off their midfield. Go and stop Paul McStay playing. Get about them. Don't let them lift their head."'

The night before the final, Nicholl called the three young players to his room to let them know they would all start the game. When Dair received the call he feared the worst. 'I got a phone call to go and see Jimmy the night before the final and I feared that I wasn't going to get picked,' says Dair.

He need not have worried. 'He told us that he was going to go with us three in the midfield,' says Dair. 'It was a brave decision for him because he obviously felt we had no fear and nothing to lose.'

Crawford recalls the moment he learned he would be starting the game, 'He pulled me, Mickey and Jason aside and said, "I want you to know that the three of you are playing. It is important that you know that I have decided to go for it. We have got to this final and sure as hell I am not losing this final by going negative." He told us and oh my God that feeling; my heart was going.'

Cameron felt the same elation. 'I knew we would be playing against the likes of Paul McStay and John Collins,' says Cameron. 'What an opportunity. I don't think we had all played together like that before, but then that is Jimmy. He had looked at their team, packed with experience in the middle of the park, then looked at us and probably thought, "You know what, I am going to put all the enthusiasm, all the energy in the middle of the park." And what we lacked in experience and know-how, we would make up for it with our energy.'

The three young players were told not to tell the rest of the squad as the announcement of the team would not be made until the following morning.

'We were going down the corridor whispering, "Brilliant, John Collins, Paul McStay, let's get into them," says Crawford. 'Right away it just got us going. Me and Jason went back to our room and were like six-year-old bairns, jumping about on these single beds, not wanting to shout in case anyone heard.'

Cameron went back to his room and phoned his father. It was a special moment for the young midfielder to be able to tell the person who had supported him most throughout his career that he would be playing in the cup final.

'When I said it to him, he said, "I told you not to give up",' says Cameron. 'He always believed in me. There was a time when I wasn't as sure as him that it was going to happen but he always believed. He was very, very proud. He couldn't wait for the game.'

The squad spent their last night before the game occupying themselves with quizzes and games.

'We just had a wee relaxing one on the Saturday night,' says Scott Thomson. 'There was a little room at the top of the hotel and the boys were playing cards and there was a dartboard. We were all sitting up there, mucking about, having a laugh and the door goes and the waiter comes in with six pints of Guinness and six pints of lager. Jimmy had obviously sent them up, so we all had a beer just to calm things down.'

The players returned to their rooms knowing that the next day they would be walking out in front of 45,000 fans in the biggest game of their Raith Rovers careers.

14

EVERY DAY IS LIKE SUNDAY

Erskine, 27 November 1994

J ASON ROWBOTHAM and the rest of the squad gathered
to hear the announcement of the team. Rowbotham had
joined Raith Rovers in 1993 after an early career with
Plymouth Argyle, Shrewsbury Town and Hereford.

'I contacted Martin Harvey who knew me at Plymouth and
Martin spoke to Jimmy and they agreed to give me a trial,' says
Rowbotham. 'I hadn't really heard of Raith Rovers and I had no
idea where Kirkcaldy was.'

The Welshman was a versatile left-back who was composed
and assured on the ball. 'I had a trial at Raith Rovers and after
the pre-season tour of Ireland, I was offered a contract,' he says.
'I moved into a flat opposite the ground on Pratt's Street. My
girlfriend, who subsequently became my wife, used to watch the
games from our bedroom window.'

The defender had been unlucky with injuries having snapped
ligaments in his knee and had been fearful that his football
career was in trouble. 'No one in England was prepared to take
a gamble on me but Jimmy Nicholl did and I owe him a lot,' says
Rowbotham.

He had joined Raith as they embarked on their first Premier Division campaign and had featured regularly in the starting 11. The presence of Julian Broddle on the left side of defence meant that the manager had a choice between the two players for the final.

Broddle was acutely aware of Rowbotham's ability and the threat he posed for the left-back position. 'Jason was a fantastic player and a great guy,' says Broddle. 'I knew him at Plymouth Argyle and he was a great lad. He always played so well when he played. He was so consistent and everything he did was right. He never put a foot wrong. It was a difficult situation to be up against him for a spot.' The atmosphere in the small, cramped room at the top of the hotel was tense as Nicholl started to read out the names of the players who would be tasked with winning the cup for Raith Rovers, 'Thomson, McAnespie, Broddle, Narey, Dennis, Sinclair, Cameron, Dalziel, Graham, Crawford and Dair. Substitutes: Potter, Rowbotham and Redford.'

It was a frustrating moment for Rowbotham. 'Jimmy named the team,' says Rowbotham. 'He hadn't said anything, he just read out the team and I was among the substitutes. I was a bit pissed off. Jimmy knew that. He'd been a player and knew the score. But at the end of the day he picked the 11 he thought would win the game, so you can't knock him.'

Rowbotham was not the only player who was disappointed. Ronnie Coyle had been struggling with fitness and was also frustrated that he would not feature in the final.

'I had been out for three months and was just getting back to fitness,' says Coyle. 'I thought I might have got a run-out before the final, even if it had been a seat on the bench. There were guys like Ian Redford getting a substitutes' place which I couldn't quite understand. That annoyed me at the time, because I knew I was fit and just needed some match practice.

'It was always going to be a struggle to make the 14 for the cup final and it is a huge disappointment in my career that I didn't make it. There won't be many players getting to a senior cup final with a team like Raith Rovers, and to miss it left a big hole.'

Davie Kirkwood, who had featured in the Ross County and Airdrie games in previous rounds, would also have to make do with a seat in the stand.

'I played at Cowdenbeath three weeks before the final and went over on my ankle,' says Kirkwood. 'I didn't play another game until the Monday before the final. That was too much of a risk so I was left out for the final. It was great to be involved though, we went away as a squad, bonuses were split and we were only there for the one thing and that was to win the cup.'

With the team announced Nicholl started to talk to his players about what this day meant. He outlined the approach to the game and then touched on how it was a chance to make history and become heroes for the Kirkcaldy club. He wanted his players to know just what a huge opportunity this was for the club, and for them, personally.

'Jimmy just started to give us the team talk and a recap of how we were going to play,' says Scott Thomson. 'Then he started going on about what it meant to us getting to the final and our families coming to watch us and how we could make history. It was quite emotional. Sinky was sitting there next to me and I'm sure he was bubbling. You were well ready for it when you came away from that.

'We didn't want to just turn up and enjoy the day. We might never get there again, so we wanted it to be a day people would remember.'

Defender Julian Broddle remembers the belief the talk instilled in the team. 'Jimmy gave this wonderful speech,' he says. 'All that was missing was the Dambusters music behind it. He was talking about each player, how wonderful they were, what great players we had, what a team we were; how we had done such an amazing thing here. How we could make history. It was the sort of talk where you felt tingling down your spine and you were thinking, "Oh my God, if I can't play in a final now then I am never going to be able to."'

On the morning of the game, the newspapers ruminated on the final that lay ahead. Most agreed that Celtic were clear favourites but a few voices questioned the mood in the Glasgow team's camp.

Ken Robertson wrote, 'A month is a long time in football. Now a seed of doubt has crept into the mind of Celtic's support as the struggling Celts have failed to produce a victory in their last eight Premier Division games.'

It was a theme picked up by ex-Rangers player Gordon Smith in his column, 'Celtic will be overwhelming favourites but they will not thank the bookies for this. They are under tremendous pressure to end their barren run of five years without a trophy. If anything, the fact that they are playing a First Division side in Raith Rovers adds to the pressure. They will realise that defeat will be greeted by nothing but derision.'

He went on to single out the Celtic captain, Paul McStay, as the player most under pressure to deliver, 'McStay has never won a trophy as Celtic's captain and he will no doubt be desperate to do so. A cup final can be a great motivator for a player or it can serve as a tremendous weight, draining the strength from his legs.'

He concluded with a bold prediction, 'Relaxation can be a powerful weapon for any team and going into the final as underdogs gives Raith a tremendous advantage. This might just be their day.'

Steve Bruce, in *The Courier*, wrote, 'A few weeks ago I thought Celtic's name was on the cup – now I am not so sure. The pressure on Celtic is enormous and if Raith can emerge from the opening 20 minutes at least on level terms, I fancy them to defy the generous-looking odds.'

Bill McFarlane at the *Sunday Post* agreed, writing, 'It's said the bookies are never wrong, but there has to be a first time for everything. That time will be 4.45 this afternoon. If Jimmy Nicholl's young braves don't freeze. 1-0 to Raith.'

The backing for the Kirkcaldy side did not go unnoticed at the team hotel. 'My mum and dad came to the hotel to pick up their tickets for the game,' says goalkeeper Thomson. 'My dad came in with all the papers and we were just having a coffee. I always remember one of the papers had various people forecasting who was going to win it and we had a few tipping us. I thought, "People are maybe fancying us here."'

The squad left their hotel to board the team bus. There were just a few hours to go until kick-off and there was nervous tension among the Rovers players. Thomson recalls a special moment as they boarded. 'We got on the bus and a couple of the boys went to sit down at the first table on the right hand side,' he says. 'Daz said, "No, no, nobody is sitting there. That is where we are going to put the cup on the way back."'

He smiles at the memory now. The team bus was joined by a police escort and as they approached Ibrox and saw the sheer volume of supporters, they knew that this was a match beyond anything they had experienced so far.

'You got closer to the stadium and you could see the amount of supporters and you were thinking, "This is the real deal now",' says Gordon Dalziel.

Nicholl lifted the tension by employing a tactic he used successfully in the Stark's Park dressing room. He cranked up the music as they approached Ibrox.

'From about a mile outside Ibrox, Jimmy put on "Simply the Best" by Tina Turner and it was turned up full,' says Jason Dair. 'Everyone was singing and banging the windows as we arrived. They must have thought we were mental!'

Davie Sinclair laughs at the memory of the squad singing along to a song so closely associated with Rangers, 'A lot of us were Celtic supporters but we were all still banging the windows. The supporters were just looking at us.'

The team arrived at Ibrox and headed inside. They had been allocated the home dressing room, a fact that amused many within the squad.

'I think it was funny because we got the home dressing room and we had a bunch of Celtic supporters in there,' laughs Stephen McAnespie. 'There was a picture of the Queen on the wall and some of the boys were heading the ball against the wall. There was a little bit of fun and games.'

Nicholl went out on to the pitch to speak to Chic Young as the first supporters took their seats. When the BBC reporter questioned the perception that Raith Rovers had nothing to lose, Nicholl replied that there was everything to lose for his players.

'I just told them there before the game at quarter to one that if they are going to settle for people coming up to them and saying, "Well you did well getting there and that is the main thing," then they will be going into this game not expecting to win,' he said. 'It is sad really because they have everything to lose. It would be a shame to think that they are not going to give everything to try and make that dream come true.'

The players took to the field to warm up as the stands started to slowly fill with supporters. The emphasis was on keeping the same routine that they had for any other game. They prepared as if they were facing Ayr United in a run-of-the-mill league match rather than Glasgow Celtic in a major cup final.

'We were just trying to stay in the routine because routine is important,' says McAnespie. 'It is how you prepare for the game. Jimmy never tried to get away from that or make us do anything different that we hadn't been doing for the rest of the season.'

The Govan Stand started to populate with Rovers fans as kick-off approached. It felt like a large slice of Kirkcaldy had turned up to witness Raith's attempt at glory. Among the 10,500 who had snapped up tickets were diehards who travelled home and away, part-timers who hadn't been to a Rovers game in years, those attending their first match, and a scattering of people whose allegiance lay elsewhere but who fancied an afternoon cheering on the underdogs from Fife.

There were fathers, sons, mothers, daughters, grandparents, friends who hadn't seen each other for years, and exiles who had travelled thousands of miles just to say they were there. For the next few hours it was irrelevant who you were or where you had come from, everyone in the Govan Stand was a Rover and that was all that mattered.

As the four sides of the stadium filled, a number of ex-Rovers were getting into position. Former players Peter Hetherston and John McStay took their seats in the Govan Stand. McStay had strong family links to the Glaswegian club but had no question marks over where his allegiance lay. 'There was never any doubt that I was going in the Raith end,' he says.

Hetherston, a Celtic fan, also found that his affection for the Kirkcaldy club and his former team-mates eclipsed any allegiance forged in childhood. 'I went to the game with a friend of Jimmy Nicholl and Jock was at the game with me as well,' he says. 'They were playing against Celtic, my boyhood heroes, but when you saw Cameron, Dair and Crawford who used to clean your boots and worked with you in training and then guys like Daz and big Ally...'

The sentence is left unfinished as he contemplates exactly what it meant to see his friends and former colleagues lining up in a national cup final.

At the far end of the ground in a makeshift *Sportscene* studio, another former team-mate, Craig Brewster, was also settling into position, having been invited by the BBC to offer his perspective on the day. He was ideally qualified to offer his assessment on exactly what it took to upset the odds in a cup final having scored the winner in the previous May as Dundee United beat Rangers to lift the Scottish Cup.

He was joined by Ally McCoist and Dougie Donnelly and they chatted amiably as kick-off approached. When asked for a prediction of who would win the match Brewster unsurprisingly felt his former team-mates could do it. 'Obviously Celtic are the favourites but I don't think Rovers have anything to fear,' he said, before adding, 'If Raith start well they have got a great chance.'

Across in the Main Stand at Ibrox sat the man who had kick-started the Kirkcaldy club nine years earlier. Frank Connor had returned to Parkhead as Celtic's reserve-team coach in June of 1994 but his role for his employers that day was peripheral, so he had taken his seat in the stand among his Celtic colleagues. 'I was with the Celtic reserves at the time, so I wasn't in the dugout or anything,' says Connor.

The former Rovers manager had mixed emotions as he waited for the game to start. His love for Celtic was absolute but he couldn't help feeling something for the club he had left in 1991. 'I was there with Celtic but my allegiances were with Raith Rovers as well,' he says. 'They protected me and my wife and family. They were my life. It was hard; you were with the club and they were a big part of you.'

As 3pm approached anticipation in the crowd intensified. Deep inside the stadium, the Rovers squad waited in the home dressing room for the call from the referee. There was a strange mix of excitement and fear with each player trying to prepare in their own way for what lay ahead. Among the younger players there was no obvious display of nerves.

'The dressing room before the game was pretty bizarre because the young guys were really cool and confident,' recalls Gordon Dalziel. 'The experienced boys like David Narey, Ian Redford, and me were more nervous than the likes of Crawford, Mickey and Jason. They treated it like it was a stroll in the park rather than a cup final. I was just sitting there thinking, "We are in a final here. Jesus Christ."'

Even with his nerves, Dalziel felt confident that his team had a chance. 'I believed in the players,' he says. 'I looked at the side and I knew we had some top quality players and a really good squad. I don't know what it was but there was something about us as guys, as a team, that made me think, "We might just get something here."'

Jason Dair felt confident. 'Because I was young it never really sunk in what we were trying to achieve,' says Dair. 'We were a First Division team against Celtic, who were Celtic! We were just going to go out and enjoy ourselves and all the pressure was on Celtic.' Stevie Crawford agreed. 'There was no fear,' he says. 'There wasn't an over-confidence; it was just a case of wanting to get the game going.'

Stephen McAnespie focused on remaining calm. 'There was such a long break in between going out to train and then going back out with all the rigmarole and walk outs and stuff,' he says. 'All of that stuff can be a little bit distracting, so keeping yourself focused for that amount of time was a little bit difficult. The boys were trying to take the edge off it, cracking some jokes here and there but for me it was just about trying to calm my nerves. I was itching to get out there.'

Finally the referee's signal came and it was time to go. 'Nicholl came and said, "Right" and I thought, "Shit." The colour just drained out of me!' laughs McAnespie.

The team left the dressing room and headed for the tunnel to line up. As they stood side by side in the Ibrox tunnel, some of the Rovers players sensed a tension in their opponents.

'We were on the right-hand side, Celtic were on the left,' says Scott Thomson. 'I felt relaxed and I felt ready for it but looking at them they didn't look relaxed. They knew they had to win this thing.'

Dalziel was also aware that his young team-mates looked more relaxed than the Celtic side. 'I looked about in the tunnel and our young boys were still laughing and joking,' he says. 'The Celtic boys must have thought, "What the hell is going on here?"'

At the front of the Celtic line was manager Tommy Burns and he approached Dalziel as they waited. 'I was standing in the tunnel and Tommy Burns walked over, put his hand out and shook my hand,' says Dalziel. 'He said, "Gordon, I would like to wish you all the best. It's great to see you." He didn't need to do that. He was under pressure and the guy was Celtic through and through and to take the time and have the decency to come over. That was a special moment.'

The teams were given the signal to begin their walk out on to the Ibrox pitch. Nicholl and Burns exchanged a final few words as they emerged from the tunnel into the deafening roar of the crowd.

As Richard Gordon waited to cover the match for BBC Radio Scotland he was taken aback by the size of the Rovers support. 'The one thing that really struck me before the game kicked off was the mass of Raith Rovers fans in that stand across from us,' says Gordon. 'It was phenomenal turnout. It was wonderful to see that. When the players came out and looked across to that it must have been so inspiring.'

Celtic may have been allocated three sides of the stadium but the first sight that both teams saw was the Govan Stand packed with supporters in blue and white. 'Walking out into that big crowd took your breath away for a second,' says McAnespie. 'When you saw the amount of Rovers fans it was pretty special.'

For players used to playing in front of crowds of two or three thousand, it was an incredible scene. It immediately gave the Rovers team a lift.

'Celtic players had to turn around and look at the main stand and the two ends,' says Ally Graham. 'But we saw our support right away and that made the old hairs on the back of the neck stand up. I'm 6ft 4in and I think some of the other boys were my height after seeing that. It was amazing, absolutely amazing.'

Crawford recalls how the turnout from the Rovers supporters made him even more determined to win. 'You walk out and that stand is all full of Raith,' he says. 'It was unbelievable. That was a massive boost. I was never focused on the crowd but when you saw that, it was back to that feeling of, "Don't let people down." If they can turn out for you in those numbers, then just make sure you don't let them down.'

The next few hours would determine whether they would or not.

15

ROLL UP YOUR SLEEVES

Ibrox Stadium, Glasgow,
27 November, 3pm

CHARLIE NICHOLAS touched the ball to Andy Walker to start the 1994 League Cup Final. It took less than a minute for Rovers to cause Celtic problems.

Stevie Crawford robbed Mike Galloway of possession just inside his own half and ran at Celtic. His pace took him beyond the midfielders and past defender Tony Mowbray. The experienced Englishman had been a late inclusion in the Celtic side having lost a stone in weight and had featured in only one of their last nine games following a virus. He was not prepared for Crawford's pace and as he realised that the young Rovers striker was beyond him, he cynically pulled him back three yards from the edge of the Celtic penalty area.

The foul denied Crawford a clear run towards goal and referee Jim McCluskey, perhaps mindful of just how early in the game it was, showed considerable leniency in failing to book Mowbray.

'I remember knocking it past Mowbray and thinking, "OK, I am going to see what you are like,"' says Crawford. 'He just takes me out. I thought the referee was soft with him, not that I wanted the player sent off, but in the manner it was done, it was a cynical foul and you think right away, "They now know they are in a game."'

Davie Sinclair was less sympathetic to the Celtic defender's predicament. 'I still think to this day, "How the hell did Mowbray not get sent off?" he says. 'He was last man and nobody was touching Crawford that day.'

The resultant free kick was rolled to an unmarked Colin Cameron who struck it well but the shot drifted a few yards wide of Gordon Marshall's goal. The game was less than two minutes old and already Rovers had made a bold statement of intent.

Rovers' sharp, precise passing frustrated Celtic in the early stages and that was demonstrated when John Collins sliced down Jason Dair in the ninth minute. It was more clumsy than malicious but it left Dair on the ground in agony. It was an injury that would keep the young midfielder out for five weeks but after the tackle he simply got up and carried on.

'I managed to play the ball wide just before John Collins tackled me and the contact twisted my knee,' says Dair. 'The adrenaline was obviously in overdrive and it never really stopped me and I never felt too much until a couple of hours after the game. There was only about a ten-minute window when it was sore though because the alcohol soon took over from the adrenaline!'

There was no sign of any inferiority complex as Rovers made a blistering start. The Raith players were throwing themselves into tackles to deny Celtic time on the ball. Shaun Dennis was his usual robust self and Sinclair bodychecked Galloway to cut off a threatening run towards the box. The uncompromising attitude was not restricted to the defence, with Stevie Crawford sprinting half the length of the pitch to stop Paul McStay in his tracks as he broke on the counter-attack.

The Kirkcaldy side were letting their more illustrious opponents know that not only could they pass the ball, they could cope with the more physical aspects of the game too.

'We couldn't haven't gone into that game and tried to sit back and hold it to 0-0,' says Cameron. 'With the energy we had in the team, in the middle of the park Jimmy just told us to get in their faces and be positive right from the word go. Not to miss out on the opportunity. Not to miss out on what was possibly there for us. We had got that far, why could we not win it?'

On the sidelines Jimmy Nicholl was pleased with the start his team had made. He had always been fearful of his players being overrun by Celtic in the opening moments.

'When you play the Old Firm you think, "I hope it doesn't end up five or six,"' says Nicholl. 'Whether it was with Dunfermline or Raith Rovers, it was the fear of losing that got me going. I thought, "I don't want this to happen today" but they settled into the cup final well. I was thinking, "We are doing all right here." I didn't have that fear anymore.'

Richard Gordon was impressed with the start that the young Rovers midfield had made. 'You got the sense that Dair, Crawford and Cameron felt at home,' he says. 'They certainly didn't seem overawed and they played really good football.'

The fast pace of the game was difficult to cope with at first for some of the players. Right-back Stephen McAnespie was finding it a challenge to adapt to the demands of the occasion. 'There was a lot of nervous energy and after the first two or three runs I was thinking, "I am knackered",' he says.

'My legs were like lead and I felt as if I had played 80 minutes. It probably took about 15 minutes to let the lactic acid get out of my legs. It was really a matter of trying to play through that and get your body attuned to the speed of the game because it was a high tempo game.'

McAnespie's task was not made any easier by the fact that he had Scottish international Tom Boyd as a direct opponent. Boyd had started the game brightly, making a couple of runs down Celtic's left.

'You are playing against international-class players,' says McAnespie. 'I have Tommy Boyd on my side and he is bombing up and down and I am supposed to be bombing up and down. It is a cat and mouse thing as we chased each other, but there were only so many runs you could do in the early part of the game with your legs being heavy.

'The fact that we had the early pressure in the game helped as it took a little pressure off the back line. We were getting the ball to our front guys and they were going and making things happen. Stevie and Mickey were taking the ball for a run here and there and creating things early. They bought us a lot of breathing space and let us acclimatise.'

Celtic hadn't started the game well but they were working hard to contain strikers Gordon Dalziel and Ally Graham. Graham was being closely tracked by Tony Mowbray.

'Mowbray was marking me and it was just a physical battle,' says Graham. 'It was a difficult game for me physically and mentally. It physically drained me and it was a number of weeks after it before I played again.'

The containment of the two frontmen meant that the most potent threat came from midfield. Crawford's early run against Mowbray had unsettled the Celtic defence and after 17 minutes, Cameron repeated the feat. The young midfielder picked up the ball from a Julian Broddle throw-in on the halfway line. As he progressed up the touchline, two Celtic defenders approached but he knocked the ball forward and sliced through them, taking them out of the game. He drove towards goal and fired in a terrific shot that flew just over Marshall's bar. The audacious piece of skill roused the Govan Stand as they roared their approval.

'That was pretty much just adrenaline,' says Cameron. 'We gained confidence from that and it was, "Look, we are causing them problems so just continue to do that."'

Celtic barely had time to recover before Cameron was running at them again. Just 60 seconds later, he picked up the ball in his own half and charged towards goal. His pace left the Celtic midfield trailing and although an attempted exchange of passes with Dalziel was blocked, the ball broke in the direction of Dair inside the box. Dair had just a glimpse of goal before Boyd arrived to clear the danger and put the ball out for a corner. There were almost 19 minutes on the clock.

The next few seconds are etched in the memory of every Raith Rovers fan who was there. Broddle delivered the corner where it found Stevie Crawford. As the Celtic defence arrived to close him down he assessed his options.

'I remember the ball coming over and just being about the edge of the box,' says Crawford. 'I took a touch, did a wee side-step and was thinking, "If I nutmeg him, I am getting a shot away." It wasn't a case of trying to nutmeg to be clever, it was just

I had a picture in my head of, "I am sliding this through his legs and then I am hitting it.'"

He managed to get the ball through McNally's legs to create a moment of space and, true to his word, fired a cracking shot towards goal. There was a mass of players inside the Celtic box and as Marshall saw the ball late, he threw out a desperate arm to stop it, but the tremendous pace and accuracy of the shot was too much for him and the ball was in the back of the Celtic net. Raith Rovers had taken the lead.

The whole Govan Stand rose to their feet and roared, screamed, clapped, punched the air, hugged and kissed in celebration. Crawford had only one thought, which was to run towards them. Most were so busy celebrating that they missed his celebration dive.

'I couldn't believe I had scored in a cup final and what a feeling running up to the stand in front of the Raith Rovers fans,' says Crawford. 'I didn't have anything in my head that if I score I am going to do this. I just took off to the side the Rovers fans were on and the Klinsmann dive was the big thing at the time, so I did the Klinsmann.'

He ran so fast that it took a moment for the rest of his team-mates to catch up. Crawford laughs as he remembers the moment. 'I do the Klinsmann and stand up and by that stage there are a few of them doing it next to me and I am standing there looking down at them thinking, "What an absolute tube I must look."'

It was an incredible moment. Not only had Raith Rovers managed to reach a cup final, they had played their Premier Division opponents off the park in the first 20 minutes and now had the impertinence to take the lead. There was a sense of disbelief all around the stadium.

'It was hysterical,' says Davie Sinclair. 'It wasn't in the script. We scored and you started to think, "We have got a chance here; we have got a right good chance."'

McAnespie was delighted, but immediately started to worry about how Celtic would react. 'I wanted the game to end right there,' he says. 'I thought, "Oh no, we have got all this time to go." I just remember thinking about the Scotland game against Brazil when Dave Narey scored and it just pissed Brazil off. I thought, "Please don't do that." I never wanted us to open up a can of worms and end up getting beaten by five goals or have a massive collapse.'

Goalscorer Crawford returned to his own half and braced himself for the expected onslaught. 'Jimmy had us prepped,' he says. 'We knew that Celtic were a good side and having played against Tommy Burns's teams at Kilmarnock, we knew that they worked hard and closed you down. So with the quality of John Collins, Paul McStay, Charlie Nicholas, Andy Walker, you knew that by scoring, you were probably going to be upsetting them.'

The Rovers bench had erupted when the goal went in and Nicholl was delighted to see his team get the reward for their excellent start to the game. 'When Stevie scored I was really enjoying the game so it was a case of, "Great, brilliant; let's see how Celtic react,"' says Nicholl.

His first priority was settling his own team down after the excitement of taking the lead. McAnespie, who was playing on the side nearest the Rovers dugout, recalls how his manager got the message to his players. 'Jimmy was on the sidelines and for the next few minutes he was shouting over, "Just settle down. Get everyone to settle. Relax,"' says McAnespie.

'He was getting the message to everyone on the field just to relax and keep ourselves in the game. It is easy to say those things but in the heat of battle it was kind of rough.'

Inevitably, the goal sparked an immediate Celtic response. From the kick-off, Boyd drove forward in a sign that the Glasgow side did not intend to stay behind for long. As they won a series of corners, the Rovers support, still high on Crawford's goal, taunted the Celtic stands with a rendition of, 'Can you hear the Celtic sing?'

Their elation was temporarily punctured when goalkeeper Scott Thomson dropped the ball in a crowded box but Thomson's defence managed to scramble the ball clear. Nicholas then found space in the box, but Dennis managed to throw his body in front of the Celtic striker's shot. Raith were struggling to win any sort of possession as Celtic applied more and more pressure. After half an hour, Collins found himself in space on the edge of the box and fired a shot in towards goal but Thomson was well positioned and collected the ball confidently.

Celtic captain McStay was beginning to impose himself on the match and dictate the pace of the game. He had struggled for the opening 20 minutes as his side's midfield failed to get to grips with the pace and energy of their three young opponents but he was now central to almost every move, winning balls in midfield and spraying passes wide to Boyd on the left.

It was from such a move that Celtic managed to fashion their equaliser. McStay created space for himself in the centre circle then skilfully delivered a pass to Boyd. The Scotland defender ran at McAnespie, and once inside the box, shot towards the goal. The whole stadium gasped as the ball beat Thomson but came back off the post and was scooped away by Dair.

The relief was short-lived as Celtic worked the ball back to Boyd who crossed dangerously towards the back post. His delivery was met by Galloway, who headed the ball back across the box to an unmarked Walker. The striker was left with the simple task of heading the ball past a helpless Thomson. Walker ran to the Celtic support with his arm raised.

Rovers had managed to hold their lead for just 13 minutes. The goal was a crushing disappointment for their supporters, but if they were being objective they could not have begrudged Celtic their equaliser on the balance of play. In the Govan Stand several small pockets of Celtic fans who had foolishly bought tickets for the Raith end, yet celebrated the goal, were being pointed out by Rovers supporters and led away by stewards.

The main focus for the Kirkcaldy team was not to concede again before the interval. 'They probably deserved their goal,' says Thomson. 'After that I was thinking, "Just get to half-time and we'll get in and get organised again." If we did that we would probably be where we wanted to be. We had scored a goal. It was level. You can't argue with that.'

The Celtic support responded to the equaliser and created an intimidating atmosphere for the next ten minutes as their side pushed for a second goal. The Rovers defence steadied themselves and managed to hold firm. Narey was a composed figure, tackling, blocking passes and breaking down moves as Celtic tried to build on their revival.

'The organisation that David Narey brought to the defence that day,' says Crawford, shaking his head. 'Jimmy must have loved it. There is only so much preparation he could give Shaun and Sinky, but having that amount of experience next to you… he was unbelievable.'

Most of the Rovers supporters were counting down the minutes to the half-time whistle and with seconds of the half left, McStay flashed a shot towards goal but it drifted wide of the right-hand post. A minute later, referee McCluskey blew his whistle and signalled half-time to the delight of everyone in blue and white.

The team were frustrated that they had lost their lead but there remained a determination not to lose the tie. 'We were disappointed at losing a goal, absolutely,' says McAnespie. 'We had battled so hard and kind of weathered the storm but at one each it was a matter of getting back out there and rolling our sleeves back up and making sure that we were still in this fight. It was still one each, we weren't getting beaten and we had 45 minutes to show we were contenders.'

The half-time period was used by Nicholl to make sure that the players realised they were still very much in the game and still had a great opportunity to win. Nicholl and assistant Martin Harvey worked on making sure that their heads did not go down.

'The management team put a lot of effort into getting people's minds back focused and focused in the right direction,' says McAnespie. 'While Jimmy was doing the overall stuff or changing the shape of the team a little bit, Harv would come around us individually. He'd give you the, "Do this a little bit differently or do this better," or whatever you required. He knew psychologically what you needed, whether it was a kick up the arse or an arm around you.

'There was a lot of disappointment at the time. If we had gone back out with the attitude we went in with, we could have crumbled very easily but when we went back out, we went back out in a positive frame of mind. It was a productive half-time.'

Nicholl made a slight adjustment to the shape of the team, moving Davie Sinclair forward in an attempt to prevent Celtic overrunning his team in midfield as they had done in the last 15 minutes of the first half. The message to the players was that the tie was very much alive, and even though Celtic would come at them in the second half it was there to be won. 'He just said, "Keep it going. We are still in with a chance,"' says Sinclair.

The players returned to the pitch focused and ready for the second half. 'It was just a case of keeping doing what we were doing,' says Cameron. 'We had conceded a goal but they were always going to get chances with the calibre of players that they had. We just had to try and limit their chances and at the same time believe that we had already scored one so we could score again.'

16

TRUE FAITH
Ibrox Stadium, Glasgow,
27 November, 4pm

ALLY GRAHAM took the ball from referee Jim McCluskey
and placed it on the centre spot. His Rovers team had
returned to the pitch first and were given a rousing
reception from the Raith support. The Celtic players emerged
from the tunnel and were greeted with an enormous roar from
their fans, who now expected their team to go on and win the
game. Gordon Dalziel put his foot on the ball and rolled it to
Graham to start the second half.

Celtic picked up from where they had left off before the break
by taking the game to the Kirkcaldy side. Within two minutes
of the restart, John Collins had tried an ambitious overhead
kick, Charlie Nicholas had fired in a shot from outside the box
and Simon Donnelly flashed a header over the bar. None of the
attempts unduly troubled Scott Thomson in the Rovers goal but
they were a sign that Celtic wanted to kill off their First Division
opponents quickly.

As Rovers' 4-4-2 formation bedded in, commentator Billy
McNeill questioned the change in tactics. 'I think Jimmy Nicholl
is taking a big, big gamble,' he said. 'He is leaving Shaun Dennis
and David Narey to account for the centre of defence and I'm

159

not convinced they are strong enough to do that.' Time would tell whether the former Celtic manager's misgivings had any foundation.

Celtic continued to press forward and on 51 minutes crafted a great chance to take the lead. Mike Galloway split the Rovers defence to find Andy Walker in space. He sprinted down the left and floated a cross into the box perfectly for the advancing Tom Boyd. With Thomson taken out of the play by Walker's cross, it looked a certain goal and as the Celtic support behind the goal rose in expectation, the Rovers fans opposite waited for the thundering roar that would greet the apparent inevitable. Incredibly, Boyd poked the ball just wide of the left-hand post while under pressure from Stephen McAnespie.

Rovers were struggling to retain any sort of possession in attack and when Graham did receive the ball after 53 minutes, he was taken down from behind by Mowbray. McCluskey finally lost patience with the Celtic defender and showed him the yellow card. If the referee had not shown such leniency towards Mowbray's brutal tackle on Stevie Crawford in the opening moments of the match, then the English defender's final would have been over there and then.

The relentless Celtic pressure continued and McStay was next to threaten, breaking into the box, but as the goal seemed to open up in front of him and he prepared to shoot, Shaun Dennis launched a great defending tackle to block the ball and it spun to safety.

The priority for Rovers during this difficult period was to hold firm. Thomson recalls the cacophony of noise from the Celtic support as their team pressed. 'The crowd was massively noisy,' he says. 'I had Celtic fans behind me at both ends, so there wasn't any respite for me but we knew that the longer the game went on, their fans would start to get a wee bit edgy with them.'

McAnespie felt it was a bruising period of the game but one which, if survived, would allow Rovers to grow in confidence. 'They really did give us a bit of a going over with the amount of possession they had,' he says. 'The second half was a battle. They were dominating play and there were two or three good moves from which they should have scored, but we showed a lot of fight and grit and determination and sometimes you make your luck and we did. We fought tooth and nail.'

Celtic had dominated since the interval but had been unable to make the breakthrough. As the game progressed with the score still level, Rovers started to look more assured. Narey and Dennis were dealing comfortably with any crosses that came their way and began to break up the waves of Celtic attacks before they truly threatened. Crawford had moved to the left and was effective in nullifying the marauding runs of Boyd which had caused Rovers so many problems in the first half.

The Rovers support, who had watched the opening 15 minutes of the second half with a foreboding sense of inevitability, realised that a Celtic goal was starting to look less and less likely. Having watched the second half in virtual silence, they began to stir and a slow, repetitive chant of, 'Come on ye Raith' began to emanate from the Govan Stand. In contrast, the Celtic support was becalmed, with some starting to audibly groan at the slightest error by their team.

'You have to remember that Celtic hadn't won anything for so long,' says Davie Sinclair. 'They must have been thinking, "We can't make a mistake here."'

The noise from the Govan Stand grew louder as the Rovers support grew in confidence. Their team had soaked up an incredible amount of pressure and was entering the final phase of the game level. As inconceivable as it had been before kick-off, there was now a real chance that they could actually win the cup. The Kirkcaldy side started to retain the ball better, won a couple of corners and looked increasingly composed.

The recovery was almost undone on the 70-minute mark when a long ball from Nicholas sent Donnelly clear. The Celtic striker looked suspiciously offside but the linesman's flag stayed down and he was through, one on one with Thomson. Donnelly hadn't scored all season and he demonstrated why when a poor second touch allowed Thomson to race from his goal and gather the ball.

As the match approached the final stages, it was evenly balanced. 'I think we got stronger as the game went on,' says McAnespie. 'It was a ding-dong battle and an evenly-matched game. We gave as good as we got and there was no way a neutral coming from a different country would have been able to tell who was the Premier Division team.'

Thomson believed that the game was heading towards extra time. 'I looked at the clock at 80 minutes and thought, "This is going to go to extra time,"' he says. 'Both teams had cancelled each other out a wee bit and the game started to slow down.'

As belief in the Rovers camp reached its peak, they fell behind. There was only six minutes remaining when Rovers tried to launch a counter-attack but it broke down and the ball found its way to Collins. He advanced forward, then chipped a pass through to Nicholas, who with the slightest of touches, helped it on to Walker.

Walker was on the edge of the penalty box with his back to goal but he pirouetted beautifully and bulleted a perfectly angled shot towards the goal. It curled inwards with Thomson beaten, but came off the inside of the post and bounced back into play. It was then the luck that Rovers had carried throughout the cup run deserted them, as it landed perfectly at the feet of Nicholas.

'I just remember going after the shot and thinking, "I'm not going to get this",' says Thomson. 'Then it came back off the post. I was just raging because it was dead lucky because anything that usually hits the post comes out the way, but it went right back across to Nicholas.'

The former Arsenal striker had built a career on his predatory instincts and despite the presence of Julian Broddle, he stabbed the ball home. 'I had just tried to come over to protect Dave Narey and Sinky,' says Broddle. 'I shouldn't have been there in the first place. It was just an absolute disaster.'

The noise around the stadium was thunderous as the Celtic support greeted the goal they had so desperately craved.

Nicholas ran to the Celtic support in the Copland Road Stand, arms aloft, and was soon swallowed up by his team-mates in celebration. As he did so, Jock Brown announced to the nation watching on television that Nicholas had, 'surely now won the cup for Celtic'.

Brown was not alone in his presumption as most wearing blue and white in the Govan Stand felt that their team had just suffered a fatal blow. *Fife Free Press* reporter John Greechan even wrote 'game over' in his notepad. There was every reason to believe that Celtic had just won the match. This tended to be the typical script for underdogs like Raith Rovers when they met either half of the

Old Firm. Turn up, perform heroically, earn the plaudits yet head home empty-handed; a mere support act to the main headliner.

Stories emerged after the game that some of the players' wives had seen a Scottish Football League official putting green and white ribbons on the cup after the Nicholas goal. It is hard to establish whether these tales are grounded in reality or myth, but at that moment it mattered little. In the minds of the Celtic team, support and most people around the stadium, the green and white ribbons might as well have been on the cup as there appeared to be no way back for the club from Kirkcaldy.

The Celtic fans raucously celebrated in the belief that their long wait for silverware was finally over and that one of their most-loved players had scored the goal to make it happen. What they didn't realise was that there was one group of people within the ground who still believed that the underdogs could get back into the game – the players wearing the dark blue shirts of Raith Rovers. 'They never took into account that we weren't finished yet,' says Graham.

Among the Rovers players, the initial emotion had been one of intense frustration at conceding a goal just as they were starting to regain a foothold in the match. 'I thought we were actually starting to play a bit better when they scored,' says Sinclair. 'It was a daft goal, a stupid one to lose, with bad marking and not picking up. It was things you learn in training all season. My heart just sank. I just thought, "Oh here we go. The dream is gone."'

Broddle felt equally despondent. 'I really felt that there was no way back but then I was never the most positive one,' says the left-back. 'I was always the pint glass is half empty and I thought, "That's it. We've played brilliantly. We can be really proud of what we've done. Nobody expected anything anyway. It will go down as a fantastic cup final."'

The goal had undoubtedly deflated the Rovers team but for most, it was a momentary, fleeting emotion. They immediately turned their attention to getting back in the game.

'For them to go and score when they did was a kick in the balls,' says McAnespie. 'For everything we had put into that half especially and the effort we put in, for that to happen was devastating, but you just had to go and pick the ball out of the net and go spot it and play. I felt we still had chances in us to go and get something, I really did. If we kept the ball moving, then with our quick guys like Mickey or Stevie, then something would open up.'

Colin Cameron was equally determined. 'I wasn't deflated,' says Cameron. 'I was disappointed but I can remember thinking, "We have worked too hard to lose this. We have only got six minutes, so we have to put everything into this last six minutes and try and get an equaliser."'

The pre-match words of Jimmy Nicholl lingered as most refused to accept the role of plucky losers who would be patronised by the media afterwards.

'If you had to come off and have people say to you, "Unlucky lads. 2-1 but you deserved something out of the game," that would have been terrible,' says Thomson. 'You don't want people to say that to you, particularly not in a final.'

As Dalziel and Graham waited to restart the match, the Rovers captain was focused on the belief that they would get one more chance. 'I remember standing at the centre spot with big Ally Graham and I said, "We have got one chance here,"' says Dalziel. 'I just knew that we were going to get a chance.'

Graham recalls the conversation, 'Daz and I took the centre and he was going to me, "Keep going. We still have time here," and I was thinking, "Fuck, there's not that much time!"'

The belief that there would be one more opportunity in the game carried the Rovers players through the next few minutes.

Nicholl had been bitterly disappointed at the loss of the goal, but he waited to see how his players would respond. 'We were holding our own and when they went ahead I thought, "Here we go again," a bit of bad luck and another hard-luck story,' says Nicholl. 'I could envisage the pats on the back in the hotel and people telling us we should be happy to get to the final in the first place.

'All you can hope for is that you have eight or nine on the pitch determined to get the situation sorted out, to get back into this game. I was just waiting to see the reaction of the boys, because I might have had to make changes right away. The reaction was good and I thought, "We are still in this."'

The Rovers manager was encouraged by how his team continued where they had left off and started passing the ball.

'We got the ball and we passed it and we passed it and we moved forward with a purpose,' says Nicholl.

He had assembled his team playing attractive, passing football and his players stuck to that philosophy in the aftermath of the Celtic goal.

'We were never a kick-and-run team,' says Stephen McAnespie. 'If we had been a kick-and-run team, we would never have got another chance and Celtic would have seen the game out. We stuck to our principles rather than starting to panic and just booting it. As much as the clock was ticking, we wanted to make sure that we had the ball. We had a lot of good players in the team who were comfortable in possession, so we stuck to our principles and kept plugging away.'

McAnespie took a quick throw-in to Sinclair halfway inside his own half. Sinclair controlled the ball on his chest and exchanged passes with Dennis before playing it back to McAnespie. With no obvious route forward, the young right-back played the ball back to Sinclair, who had made space for himself in the centre circle. He played the ball back to Narey who swept it out to Broddle on the left. The left-back knocked it up to Crawford, who immediately returned it, allowing Broddle to find Cameron.

Cameron knocked it back to Narey who returned it forward to the young midfielder. As Cameron turned to start his run forward, McStay clipped him and the referee awarded a free kick. It was a remarkable display of composed, passing football as the seconds on the clock ticked away towards full time. The stadium was still electrified from the Celtic goal and the Glasgow side's supporters were in full voice as Narey readied to take the free kick.

There were five navy blue shirts in the box, with a further three sitting just outside, as Narey flighted the ball in. The ball reached the head of Brian O'Neill who cleared it, but only as far as Sinclair. The Rovers player controlled the ball and skilfully wrong-footed Collins to buy himself some space and time. He used it to pass the ball out to Dair on the right.

'The ball breaks out and I take a touch and play it to Jason,' says Sinclair. 'I thought he was going to take him on and run him to the byline but he had a shot and the rest is history.'

Crawford smiles as he recalls the run and shot from his friend. 'Jason cut in and hit that left-foot shot. He always says he had a bit of movement on it but I am not giving him that,' he laughs. 'It is not even a great shot. There is no power in it or nothing.'

Dair cut inside two players and let fly with his left-foot shot. As it made its way towards goal, Dalziel used his years of experience to follow it in. 'I saw him going to have a shot and I thought to myself that if you don't buy a raffle ticket, you will never win the raffle!' says Dalziel.

'You've got to take a wee gamble. I thought, "Well, the minute he hits that my instinct is go in." It was years of being a goalscorer and thinking the ball is not dead until it is out of the park or in the goalie's hands. Mowbray and McNally were the centre-backs that day and they switched off as they thought that Marshall was collecting Jason's shot.'

Gordon Marshall didn't collect the shot. Inexplicably, he fumbled the ball which bounced up into the path of the advancing Dalziel. At the far end of the pitch, Thomson watched the move unfold.

'I was watching and could see the build-up,' he says. 'I could see Jason cutting in, cutting in and I was thinking, "Go and just hit it," and he did. It wasn't one of Gordon Marshall's best saves and Daz was just there doing what Daz does, being in the right place at the right time.'

The game seemed to almost pause for a moment as Dalziel reached the ball and, with Marshall still on the ground, headed it into the empty net. Unbelievably, just three minutes after conceding a goal, Raith Rovers had equalised.

'Fortunately the ball bounced up off the keeper and presented me with a tap-in from five yards,' says Dalziel. 'It was like slow motion, just trying to get the ball into the back of the net. It wasn't the best goal that I ever scored, but it is probably the most important goal that I have ever scored.'

It was vintage Dalziel, knowing where to be at exactly the right moment. His instinctive positional sense was why he had been signed for Rangers as a youth and why he had become Rovers' all-time leading scorer, but of his 170 goals for the Kirkcaldy club, there was none more important.

'Daz made that chance look easy because he gambled,' says Crawford. 'He was unbelievable and he had a belief that he was going to score. How many players would actually have followed in there in a cup final?'

Behind the goal was club photographer Tony Fimister. It was sheer luck that he was at that end. 'You had to pick your spot before the game and you weren't allowed to move,' says Fimister. 'If you sat there, you were there for the whole game. When Dalziel scored that goal, I had obviously got a shot of the goal, but I punched the air in celebration and hit the photographer next to me; smacked him in the head. Then I realised that I had thousands of Celtic fans right at my back! It was an unbelievable feeling and the noise from the Govan Stand was unbelievable.'

The roar from the Rovers support as Dalziel bundled the ball into the net was incredible. They could scarcely believe what was happening, having been utterly despondent minutes earlier when Nicholas had scored. There were stunned looks of disbelief everywhere as they embraced in the stand.

'I just remember that wall of Raith Rovers fans,' recalls Richard Gordon. 'The emotion; the excitement; everything came spilling out from them and just the silence around the rest of the ground, looking around and seeing the deflation.'

Dalziel ran to the side of the pitch but was faced with a wall of Celtic fans. 'I turned and all I could see were Celtic supporters everywhere but what a feeling,' he says.

He stared them down as he celebrated his goal and was embraced by his jubilant team-mates. Never one to miss an opportunity, as he made his way back to the halfway line, he pointed towards the Main Stand packed with Celtic supporters and re-enacted his goal. 'I kidded on that I was heading the ball,' he says. 'Then I shouted up to them, "That is what I am fucking all about." I don't know where it came from.'

It was an unbelievable moment of redemption for the Rovers striker. Just eight years earlier he had been on the verge of quitting football having fallen out of love with the game, until Frank Connor arrived on his doorstep. Now he was scoring an improbable equaliser for his side in front of 45,000 fans in a national cup final. Dalziel deserved his moment.

In the commentary box Dalziel's former strike partner Craig Brewster was ecstatic. 'You can imagine what it was like in the commentary box with someone who had been with Raith Rovers a year previously and a Rangers man,' says Brewster. 'You can imagine the excitement. It was quite a sight to see. I remember saying to McCoist later on that when Daz scored the equaliser I thought it had come off his nose and McCoist quick as a flash said, "If it had come off his nose it would have burst the net."'

The belief that Dalziel scored with his nose still lingers to this day, although for the sake of historical accuracy it was definitely his head. The rest of the Rovers team didn't care what part of his body Dalziel had used, they were back in the game.

'My first thought was, "Shit, we've got another 30 minutes of this,"' laughs McAnespie. 'I wasn't sure how my legs would hold up to it but obviously you are hoping it happens and then suddenly it does. Everyone was looking at the linesman, "Is he offside?" We were waiting on something happening.

'You have got to remember we were playing Celtic in a cup final and it was the last few kicks. You are thinking, "Are they going to chop this off just because they are the big guys and we are the little guys?" It would be easy to do. All those things run through your mind in a split second. And then suddenly he was pointing at the centre spot and it's a goal and it is game on again.'

In the chaos of the equaliser, fellow defender Julian Broddle can't recall exactly how he celebrated Dalziel's goal but he knows his mind would have been on trying to regain his composure for the remainder of the game.

'I would have been trying to get my second breath or third breath or fourth breath,' he jokes. 'I was never one for running around at goals. When I scored goals myself, I never ran around as I was always too knackered. I would have liked people to have lifted me up and carried me back and put me back in my position! So when Daz scored I would have been overjoyed but walking as slowly as possible to get back to where I was supposed to be to try and get my breath back.'

BBC reporter Chic Young had missed the goal as he was making his way from the Ibrox gantry to trackside. 'It was 2-1 to Celtic and I was told to make my way down towards the tunnel to prepare for the post-match interviews,' he recalls. 'I came up the tunnel and there was no sign of a victory. The game was raging on. I said, "What happened?" Raith Rovers had equalised and I had missed the goal! I wondered why I wasn't interviewing Celtic players.'

Tommy Burns would later describe the Raith equaliser as a moment that 'tore the heart out of everyone' at Celtic. The man who had caused such distress saw the impact for himself. 'I remember going back for the restart and the look on the faces of Tony Mowbray and Mark McNally said it all,' says Dalziel. 'They were absolutely sick. I definitely think that was the turning point for us.'

The game resumed with only three minutes remaining. Celtic pushed forward and forced a corner. Collins made his way into the box and fired a low shot but McAnespie was in position on the post and watched it drift wide. The Celtic support grew impatient with their team and a long pass back to Marshall was met with incessant whistling and loud boos.

As the match ticked into injury time, the Rovers support struck up another chorus of 'Can you hear the Celtic sing?' but just as they did, Mike Galloway robbed Crawford deep inside his own half and steamed forward supported by four team-mates.

Galloway tried to force the ball wide to Donnelly but overhit it and left the youngster no chance. Donnelly blasted the ball against the advertising hoarding in frustration and a further barrage of boos rang out from the Celtic support.

It was to be the last action of the 90 minutes as Jim McCluskey blew the final whistle. The game had finished 2-2 and Rovers had earned another half an hour. Their support greeted the whistle with a huge collective sigh of relief. Around the rest of the ground the Celtic fans let their team know what they thought of them surrendering their winning lead with more jeers.

It had been a hugely entertaining and competitive final and as both teams prepared for extra time, the Raith Rovers players and support knew that in one sense they had already won. After being down and out after 84 minutes they had fought back to take the game into extra time. Among the players one thought dominated, 'We can go on and win this.'

17
JUST A TOUCH AWAY
Ibrox Stadium, Glasgow,
27 November, 4.55pm

JIMMY NICHOLL was startled by a loud cheer as he returned to the dugout in preparation for extra time. The cheers had emanated from the Kirkcaldy support as they watched a replay of the Gordon Dalziel goal on the large screens in the corners of the stadium installed by Coca-Cola. In the commentary position Billy McNeill heaped praise on the Kirkcaldy side as he waited for the game to restart.

'I have got to be honest,' he said. 'I thought that would have killed Raith Rovers. I had a look at the expressions on their faces when Nicholas put that goal in but they have been a marvellous example of First Division football.'

Celtic won the toss and elected to let their opponents kick off. The loss of a late goal had been a devastating blow for the Parkhead club and their disappointment was evident in extra time where they struggled to impose themselves on the game or create any real scoring opportunities.

The quick transition from elation to deflation seemed to sap the Celtic players of energy and belief and it was Raith Rovers who started briskly and passed the ball comfortably at the start of extra time.

'I felt, in extra time, we grew in confidence and if anybody was going to win it then it was going to be us,' says Colin Cameron. 'That equaliser seemed to knock the stuffing out of them and it was the opposite for us. It gave us a wee bit of renewed energy.'

Stephen McAnespie agrees, 'I felt we dominated extra time. I think we had the better of the play. I think we became stronger and we were more composed.'

Former Rovers manager Frank Connor saw that Celtic had lost belief and were starting to struggle. 'The Rovers were up for it and after Dalziel had scored, the Raith Rovers players got a lift,' says Connor. 'When it went to extra time Celtic could have done anything and they wouldn't have scored, the way the game was going.'

The frantic 90 minutes had taken its toll on most of the players and Rovers were the first to make a substitution when Jason Rowbotham was brought on to replace the struggling Julian Broddle. 'I was chasing for a ball into the corner and my leg went,' says Broddle. 'It was totally gone. I couldn't wait to get off because I was knackered and I didn't fancy being a penalty taker. I just didn't want to get involved in that.'

Having been frustrated at being left out of the starting 11, Rowbotham was pleased to be given the opportunity to make a contribution to the game. 'It was amazing to be involved in a national cup final,' he says. 'When I came on as a sub, I didn't want to let anyone down.'

He was roundly booed by the Celtic support who mistakenly believed that he was former Rangers player Ian Redford. Rowbotham's first involvement was to concede a free kick just outside the box. Paul McStay went down easily and the Welsh defender was quick to make his thoughts known as he shook his head and smiled wryly at the Celtic skipper.

The attempted cross from the set piece was blocked by Davie Sinclair, who chased down the rebound and won back possession. Sinclair was starting to assert himself on the game with his willingness to win challenges and break up play. He even managed to take out both Collins and McStay simultaneously in one robust tackle. At times his elegant passing and composure on the ball resembled a Fife Franz Beckenbauer.

Ally Graham picked up only the second booking of the game for a late challenge on Tom Boyd although it appeared to owe more to tiredness than malicious intent.

Rovers were dominating possession and looking increasingly dangerous on the break. A beautiful flowing move involving an audacious Dalziel back-heel to Stevie Crawford ended in the striker sending a stinging shot towards Marshall, who held it at the second attempt. A sense of belief was growing on the Rovers bench.

'The first time I thought we had a chance was in extra time,' says kitman John Valente. 'In extra time I was sitting down and I heard Martin Harvey turning around after 15 minutes and saying to Jimmy, "You know Jimmy, we have got a chance." And I thought to myself, "Jesus Christ so we have."'

Nicholl agrees that his side grew in strength in the additional half an hour. 'I think I have seen the game once in the last 20 years and if my memory serves me right we should have won that in extra time,' says Nicholl.

Charlie Nicholas was withdrawn as he visibly tired, to be replaced by Paul Byrne. Dalziel limped off to be replaced by Redford. The pace of the game dropped and when Crawford went down with cramp, it gave both sets of players a much needed break.

As the match approached its conclusion, the atmosphere in the stadium crackled and tension increased as both teams feared losing a late goal.

'I think, looking back, it would probably have been unfair if someone had got something in extra time,' says Stephen McAnespie. 'The game had been so much back and forth, for someone to win it in extra time would have been harsh.'

With the seconds counting down and the Rovers support whistling for the match to end, Celtic finally emerged from their torpor and mounted their first real threatening attack in the additional period. Mike Galloway sprinted to the byline and lofted over a cross. None of his team-mates could reach the ball but they did enough to pressurise Stephen McAnespie into heading the ball behind for a corner.

The match had slipped into injury time as Byrne prepared to take the corner. In the Govan Stand supporters held their breath and some couldn't watch as the ball was swung in. Their team had battled for 120 minutes and the least they deserved was a chance to win on penalties. To lose a goal now would have been the cruellest of blows.

Thankfully, the in-swinging cross was met by Galloway at the near post, but his header was aimed into the side netting. At the far end, some Celtic supporters thought he had scored as they saw the side net bulge and the Rovers support mocked their mistake with a mixture of amusement and relief.

Scott Thomson passed the ball to McAnespie who launched it upfield and there were loud, relived cheers from the Rovers support as the referee blew his whistle. The 1994 League Cup Final would be decided by penalty kicks.

The Rovers team hugged and congratulated each other as they gathered in the centre of the pitch. There were handshakes and the occasional embrace for some of the Celtic players, reflecting the positive spirit in which the game had been played. The first problem was that the allocation of tickets meant that whichever end was chosen it would be Celtic fans behind the goal.

'When it went to penalties, I felt as if it was going to be harder for Raith Rovers as there were Celtic supporters behind both goals,' says Rowbotham. 'So whatever end was chosen, we were going to be kicking the ball down their throats.' The Broomloan Road Stand was selected as the end where the final would be decided.

The players tried to prepare themselves for what lay ahead; the majority gulping liquid in a bid to rehydrate after a punishing 120 minutes of effort. Some had their legs massaged in an attempt to loosen stiff limbs while others tried to pick out loved ones in the stands.

'It is just a matter of getting yourself prepared and making sure that you don't get in each other's way,' says McAnespie. 'You see a couple of guys walking away and going off by themselves and doing their own thing to get mentally prepared. It is just a matter of trusting and believing in each other to make sure you get the job done.'

The team had practised penalties a couple of days before the final but nothing could adequately prepare them for the atmosphere they were about to face inside Ibrox. The manager barely had to intervene as the order of penalty takers was established. He had his volunteers quickly: Shaun Dennis, Jason Dair, Colin Cameron, Stevie Crawford and Stephen McAnespie.

'You are just looking for them to step up,' says Nicholl. 'You just calm them down and get the order, then it is up to them. They were always quick to volunteer so that wasn't a problem and they were all comfortable with who was taking penalties when. I just said to them, "You have been brilliant to get to this position. You did great in extra time and maybe should have won it but you haven't, but now we can go and win it on penalties. Gather your thoughts. You are all right. You are going to do it."'

Thomson exchanged words with Brian Potter then drifted to the edge of the main group to prepare mentally. The hero from the semi-final shoot-out hoped that history would repeat itself in the final. 'I just wanted Scott to experience what I had experienced, but on a much bigger level,' says Potter.

As Nicholl left the pitch to return to the dugout, he had no fear for his players and his overwhelming emotion was pride. 'All credit to the players,' says Nicholl. 'They kept digging in and did not abandon their passing game. In extra time I felt we were perhaps the stronger side and fully deserved to be still in the frame at the end of 120 minutes. It was easy to watch the penalties because I was proud of them.

'Nobody could ever say to them, "Well, you just had a day out. You just showed up. You never showed what you were capable of producing," and let the occasion get to them. It never got to them.'

Rovers won the toss of the coin and elected to go first. They knew from their experience in the semi-final that going first was a significant advantage, but only if they scored their penalties. As the shoot-out was about to begin, the Celtic support attempted to imbue their side with confidence with a sea of green and white scarves and a chorus of, 'You'll Never Walk Alone'.

Dennis was the first Raith player up. 'Shaun was always really cool,' says Cameron, and the big defender proved it by sending Gordon Marshall the wrong way and putting Rovers 1-0 ahead. Dennis responded to the loud Celtic jeers that had accompanied his walk to the penalty spot by holding out his hands in a 'What have you got to say now?' gesture. Dennis was followed by substitute Willie Falconer, who emulated the Rovers man by curling the ball into the right-hand side of the goal. After two penalties it was level at 1-1.

Dair was next for Rovers. He placed the ball on the spot and walked back to his starting position. His penalty wasn't the most convincing and with Gordon Marshall guessing the right way there was a brief moment of alarm among the Rovers support, but the ball crept under the goalkeeper's arms and into the net to make it 2-1 to Raith.

'Walking up I can't remember being that nervous,' says Dair. 'I was always going to keep it low and decided on the way up, to put it to my right. It wasn't exactly in the corner but sneaked under Gordon Marshall's arms and I could breathe again.'

Nicholl recalls his young striker's penalty with slightly less confidence. 'Jason Dair's was the worst one,' says Nicholl. 'I didn't actually realise on the day how close it was to being saved. It was only when I looked back on it a few days afterwards you think, "Phew," but fortunately he scored.'

In the Ibrox tunnel Gordon Dalziel waited beside Chic Young from the BBC, unable to watch. 'It was just like the semi-final. I didn't watch the penalty shoot-out against Airdrie and it was the last thing on my mind to watch this one,' says Dalziel. 'I was in the tunnel and Chic Young was winding me up. All I could see were the Raith Rovers supporters and I knew by their reaction if we had scored.'

Collins was next for Celtic and confidently placed his shot in the left-hand corner, sending the goalkeeper the wrong way. He had looked calm on his approach but as he jogged back to the centre circle a thankful glance towards the heavens revealed just how relieved he was to have levelled the score at 2-2.

Thomson was frustrated with himself that he hadn't come close to saving either of the first two penalties. 'I had said to Brian Potter, "The first two I am going to go to my right" and I changed my mind,' he says. 'I was annoyed and wondering why I changed.'

Cameron walked forward to take Rovers' third penalty. 'In the game I was so focused I could have been playing in an empty stadium,' says Cameron. 'To me it was just a constant drum, nothing specific, just like a noise you hear in the back of your mind but on the walk up I was aware of the crowd for the first time. It took me about 20 minutes to get there. It was a long walk, to be honest. I was just thinking, "This is where I am putting it. I am not changing my mind."'

By the time Cameron reached the ball, his mind was back refocused on the task in hand. 'Behind the goals there were Celtic fans but all I saw was Gordon Marshall in the goal,' he says. 'You didn't want to be the one who missed. No one remembers who takes the penalties, they always know who misses. He went the right way but it went in the side net so I don't think any goalkeeper could have saved that. There was a great feeling of relief after it.' It was a terrific penalty and it edged Rovers back in front 3-2.

Goalscorer Andy Walker strode forward for Celtic's third kick. He had been a regular penalty taker throughout his career and it showed as he calmly fired the ball down the middle of the goal. The tension was increasing as the shoot-out neared the final takers with the score tied at 3-3.

On the touchline, Nicholl was impressed by his players' strength of character in such a demanding situation. 'They were so confident,' he says. 'You could see it in them, they were just enjoying the occasion and enjoying the fact they'd taken Celtic right to the wire.'

If the stakes were getting progressively higher then it didn't feature in the thinking of Crawford as he stepped forward for Rovers' fourth penalty. 'I never thought about missing it when I was going up,' says Crawford. 'It never entered my head. It was just a moment of pure concentration. You never thought for one minute what would have happened if you were the one to have missed the penalty or what dream you were killing.'

As he struck the ball Marshall dived the right way but the shot crept under his arms and into the net. Crawford reflects now on the quality of his penalty. 'My penalty and Jason's weren't the greatest of efforts,' he laughs. 'Looking back, Gordon Marshall could probably have saved both of them but they sneaked under him. What a relief for both of us.'

The shoot-out was following the pattern of the semi-final with Rovers increasing the pressure on their opponents with each kick. As Rovers led 4-3, Cameron sensed that events were working to his team's advantage. 'When Craw's and Jason's went in, I turned around and said to Sinky, "We are winning this",' says the midfielder. 'I just had a gut feeling.'

Paul Byrne was next for Celtic. The young Irishman had come on as a substitute in extra time but had failed to make any significant contribution to the match. He hurriedly approached the ball and looked anxious to take his penalty. His haste was rewarded as he confidently sent Thomson the wrong way to level the scores at 4-4.

There were now just two penalties left if the final was to be decided in the first ten kicks and the Celtic support raised the volume as they sensed that the shoot-out was reaching a critical stage. As Stephen McAnespie started his walk towards the goal the noise level increased, rising to a deafening crescendo of boos and jeers from the Celtic fans.

'I can safely say that was the longest walk of my life,' says McAnespie. 'You don't know whether to run. You don't know whether to skip. You don't know whether to walk. You don't want to look stupid on your way up there because you know you are on TV! It feels like an eternity and once you are up there then there is no turning back. It is like being on a rollercoaster: once you are sitting in it and locked in, you can't get back out.'

As the fifth penalty taker for the Kirkcaldy side, the young right-back was acutely aware of the pressure he was under. He knew that a miss could cost his side the cup. 'If you are at the start or nearer the middle, then you still have opportunities to get it back,' he says. 'If I miss it is over. OK they still have to score but if I miss we are done. No one says anything, but in your own mind you're counting the numbers and you think, "It is on my shoulders."

'I walk up and try to have a little look around, take a deep breath and take in the atmosphere and try and disregard that part of it but it is hard. It is prevalent; it is there. It is a reality that if I miss, then I'll never be able to show my face in Kirkcaldy again.'

He glanced at the referee then began his run-up. He had already decided that his tactic was to hit the ball as hard as he could towards the middle of the goal.

'I was never one of these guys who tried to side-foot it in the corner or do this or that. It is getting crashed down the middle,' he says. 'And if the goalkeeper stands there and saves it, fair play to him, but if he dives in any direction then there is no chance of saving it. That is the principle as far as I was concerned. Get up there and get the business done.'

McAnespie got the business done. As Marshall dived to his left, the defender's penalty blasted into the net. McAnespie punched the air with relief. Rovers had scored all their five penalties just as they had in the semi-final and led 5-4. They were now only one kick away from winning the cup and from qualifying for European competition.

The tension around the stadium was virtually unbearable and Celtic manager Tommy Burns looked pallid with anxiety as he watched Mike Galloway step forward for the final penalty. Galloway hit the ball to the right and for the first time Thomson guessed correctly. The crowd inside Ibrox gasped as the goalkeeper got a hand to the ball but it managed to wriggle its way underneath and crossed the line to make it 5-5.

The Celtic fans immediately realised just how close they had come to losing and burst into song, fuelled by a curious mix of defiance and relief. Thomson was left frustrated that he couldn't get enough of a hand on the ball to keep it out. 'I guessed right when Mike Galloway stepped up and the ball hit the underside of my hand and squeezed in,' he recalls. 'I thought then it was going to be one of those days for us.'

With the first ten penalties successful it was now up to the players who had not initially volunteered. Many of the Rovers players were feeling the pressure of the occasion. 'It was working its way down to me,' says Ally Graham. 'I was like that, "Somebody do something here," because I didn't want to take a penalty.'

Davie Sinclair was equally nervous. 'I wasn't looking forward to it,' says the defender. 'I could take penalties in training and they were easy but not in front of 40,000 people. That takes a lot of bottle.'

The player whose 'bottle' would be tested was substitute Jason Rowbotham. The Welshman recalls the moment his name was put forward. 'The first five were all organised, then someone said, "Woofer will take one." Woofer was my nickname,' says Rowbotham. 'Jimmy turned round and saw everyone turning away from him. He said, "You're on the next one" and I thought "cheers".'

What Rowbotham had failed to tell his manager and team-mates was that his record in taking penalties wasn't exactly impressive. 'I didn't tell anyone but I'd only taken one penalty in senior football up until that point in a Plymouth Argyle reserve match and I missed!' he laughs.

As he approached the penalty spot there was bedlam all around Ibrox. The Celtic fans were doing their utmost to break his concentration and willing him to miss. 'I tried to stay focused,' he says. 'There was pressure on me to put us back in front. The boys had worked so hard during the 90 minutes and extra time that I didn't want to let them down.'

Rowbotham kept his composure and made no mistake, sending Marshall the wrong way. 'I was a relieved man,' he says. 'I passed it in, really. If the keeper had gone the right way it would have been a nice height for him. Fortunately he didn't.'

As Rowbotham jogged back to re-join his team-mates in the centre circle he clapped the Rovers support and glanced to his left to see Paul McStay approaching for Celtic. Rovers led 6-5 and it was now up to the Celtic captain to keep his team in the match.

18

ECSTASY
Ibrox Stadium, Glasgow, 27 November, 5.20pm

SCOTT THOMSON waited for McStay to arrive. He was frustrated that he hadn't gotten closer to the previous five penalties and was determined to save this one. He remembered the advice that Brian Potter had given him earlier.

'Potts had said to me before, "At one of the penalties just throw the ball up in the air. Get them thinking for a minute," and I hadn't done that,' says Thomson. 'So I saw Paul McStay coming up and thought, "Right, I need to do it this one." We were in sudden death and I thought, "Something has got to change here. I need to break up the routine."'

He threw the ball in the air and returned to his line. The fact that he was facing the Celtic captain made no difference to the Raith keeper, his only thought was saving the penalty. 'You are not really looking at who it is,' says Thomson. 'You know who is taking it but it doesn't matter. You just need to make the save.'

As McStay had made his walk forward some started to sense a tension in the Celtic captain. Behind the goal, photographer Tony Fimister was lining up his next picture. 'At the penalty I'm lined up but I was looking above the camera because I knew I wasn't going to be taking the shot just yet. I looked and his legs were like rubber. You could tell he was scared,' he said.

Fimister wasn't the only one who sensed the Celtic captain's nervousness. 'I had no confidence in him whatsoever,' says Stephen McAnespie. 'He looked sheepish. He looked nervous. He looked as if he just did not want to be there. It was as if he was taking the penalty simply because of who he was.

'He looked as if he had been bullied to go up there to fulfil his obligation to Celtic and it was a bad place for him to be. If you watch him in the video, his head is never up. He is within himself. He was always introverted and nervous about it.'

Davie Sinclair recalls the conversation in the centre circle as McStay approached the ball. 'We were standing talking about Paul McStay because he's not a natural pinger of a ball,' says Sinclair. 'One of us said, "He's missing this."'

McStay started his run and hit the ball to Thomson's right-hand side. Thomson guessed correctly and moved towards the ball. 'I had made up my mind the way I was going because I had come close to stopping Galloway's kick,' he says. 'Right-footers normally put it to the right, so I just dived the full length to my right.'

Fimister recalls his unusual view of the moment. 'When he hit it I was concentrating on my shot, which was fixed, but out of the corner of my eye I could see the keeper flying across and I thought, "He's got it!"' says Fimister. 'I'm still looking at McStay and his eyes went wide open in shock.'

The Celtic captain had just watched Thomson reach the ball and push it away from the goal. McStay slumped to the ground and buried his head in his hands, knowing that his penalty had just been saved.

'It was like everything stopped,' says Thomson. 'It is a moment that will stay with me forever. That is why you play football. That is why you want to be there.'

Raith Rovers had won the League Cup and Thomson started to sprint away but appeared uncertain as he glanced back at the referee. 'There was a delay because the referee, Jim McCluskey, pointed at me and I thought he was signalling for a retake but then I realised he only wanted the ball back,' he says. 'I just can't describe the feeling. It was just a case of where am I going to run? I just ran towards the centre circle but the rest of the boys had run to the Rover's support so there was nobody there by the time I got there!'

Around the stadium there was chaos. The seemingly impossible had just become a spectacular reality. In the centre circle Thomson's team-mates couldn't quite believe what they had just witnessed.

'We were standing looking directly at the goal,' says Ally Graham. 'You couldn't really see the angle of the ball. We couldn't tell whether the ball had gone under his body or squirmed into the net and it wasn't until he reacted that I knew he had saved it. Then all hell broke loose. It was like The Red Arrows, everyone was just running about daft.'

The players sprinted in every direction possible. 'I remember being told to stay in the centre circle no matter the outcome of the penalties,' says Jason Dair. 'But when we won, everyone just bolted to our family and friends in the Main Stand or the Raith fans in the stand opposite, to celebrate with them.'

Brian Potter recalls being given the same instructions on the touchline. 'I am sure there were police and stewards there saying stuff like, "You can't do this or that",' says Potter. 'Nobody was going to stop managers, coaches and players running on the park. You can have all the protocol you want but the emotions just go to your head.'

Stephen McAnespie describes the joy of the moment. 'You normally see a team that wins all jump on each other,' says the defender. 'We all ran in different directions. It was pandemonium. It was just disbelief to think that we had just achieved that. We had beaten Goliath.'

The feeling among the Rovers players was one of elation that they had managed to not only reach the final but win the cup.

Stevie Crawford was struggling to take it in, 'He saved the penalty and I'm thinking, "I love Scott. I love him." Then, "My God, Jimmy is our manager and I'm playing with mates. I am not just playing with boys that are being paid money to play football. These are my mates!" And all the fans are there. I just thought, "Jesus". You realised what it meant to everybody, the closeness, to celebrate a victory like that and the friendships that we had built.'

Even today Colin Cameron struggles to put the moment into words. 'It is indescribable to be honest with you. It was just pure elation,' he says. 'All the hard work we put in through the course of the previous games…we had come up against some hurdles where it might not have been, but that is what makes you successful. You are able to come up against these things, the setbacks, and just have a constant belief that we were able to deal with it.'

Raith Rovers had just won the League Cup and no one could quite believe it. As the Celtic supporters immediately started to leave the stadium, the Rovers support celebrated in disbelief at what they had just witnessed. There had been an explosion of noise from the Govan Stand as Thomson saved the penalty.

'The atmosphere at Ibrox that day was incredible,' says Cameron. 'The fans were wonderful because they were outnumbered three to one but gave us great backing.'

Sinclair agrees, 'It was just joy, sheer joy, not just for us but for those guys in the stands watching us. I had all my family there; my mum and dad. Words can't describe my feelings that day. I was so overwhelmed with emotion. I stood on the halfway line and cried my eyes out. I couldn't believe we'd won the cup.'

Jimmy Nicholl would later joke that Sinclair was crying despite being so tough that he had 'tattoos on his teeth'. If Sinclair was struggling to control his emotions then so was the Rovers manager.

'When I saw Thommo looking at the referee I thought he must know that he moved early or something, so there is going to be a retake,' says Nicholl. 'Once we knew it was all right, it was just, "Whoosh". I just remember running on the park; sprinting out like a madman with my arms up. I don't think I even ran to anybody, I just ran. It was so emotional. That was when I let my emotions go, when I thought these lads, who were part-time players two or three years before, were going to Europe. Brilliant.'

Nicholl was quickly grabbed by Chic Young for an interview but was too emotional to speak. 'I am speechless, I can't say anything,' he told Young. Young persisted and asked how he felt, to which an exasperated Nicholl replied, 'How do you think I feel?' before leaving to congratulate his players.

The exchange was a fraught one for the BBC reporter. 'I had the director of the programme in my ear screaming, "Let's go to Chic, he's got the manager",' recalls Young. I said to him "Jimmy, what have you got to say?" and he said, "I can't say anything." The director in my ear said, "He'll need to say fucking something. We've got two minutes to fill!" Jimmy was trying to run away from me and I was hanging on to him, wrestling with him. He was just so emotional.'

'Everything had built up,' recalls Nicholl. 'Everything I had been thinking about for the club, the cup, the European thing. It was all going to happen. It was unthinkable. You couldn't imagine that Raith Rovers could go on and win it and get into Europe, and that was the most important thing for me.

'People say to me, "Jimmy it must have been great beating Celtic because you were a Rangers man," but that wasn't the thing for me, it was getting Raith Rovers into Europe.'

The cold, hard fact was that Raith Rovers were in Europe. A small club like Raith would take their place in the following season's UEFA Cup alongside the elite of European football. It was almost laughable.

Paul McStay and the rest of the Celtic team remained on the pitch as Rovers celebrated. Their punishment was to linger in the glare of their fans for a few minutes longer. His team-mates attempted to console and reassure their captain.

Reflecting back on McStay's plight now, there is sympathy from his opponents. 'You look back at it and think even though he was a legend and a Scotland international and an unbelievable player, the pressure on his shoulders going up to take that penalty must have been unbelievable,' says Cameron.

'He was probably going up there thinking, "I am the captain of the best club in the country, playing against a First Division club and if I miss this, they have beat us." We had none of that. We had no pressure. We weren't expected to win but for him it had obviously proved too much.'

Afterwards the Celtic captain would comment on his miss. 'When it was my turn, I took it. The keeper guessed right and saved it and that's it,' he said. 'I was not in the first five because others were more used to it but in sudden death it was my responsibility to go on first turn. It didn't work and that's something I have to live with.' He added ruefully, 'The game should never have gone to penalties. It should have been won in the 90 minutes.'

Reflecting back on it now, McStay is philosophical about the events of that afternoon. 'Scott did his job on the day,' he says. 'He saved my penalty and Raith Rovers achieved their objective and were worthy winners on the day. Jimmy and Frank were excellent coaches and deserve a lot of praise for the way they built the team over the years and they were rewarded for their hard work.'

John McStay was delighted that Rovers had won but regretted that it was his cousin that had missed the vital penalty. 'When I saw Paul walking up, I knew he was going to miss it,' says John. 'I just had a feeling, I don't know why. The only thing I would change about the cup final would be that it wasn't Paul that missed the penalty. Anyone else missing it would have been fine.'

Celtic coach Frank Connor has tremendous sympathy for the player. 'He was one of Celtic's best players,' says Connor. 'He was a great guy; quiet, unassuming, but then that's life. On another day, if you're blessed it could have been different. I think it worked out well in the end. It was great for Raith Rovers. It was great for the crowd and it was great for the players and for the town. Celtic would get bits and pieces later on.'

The disconsolate Celtic players received their medals and headed straight for the tunnel. Some of their fans were angered by their team's performance and discarded their scarves in a gesture of displeasure.

Tommy Burns later commented on the impromptu protest in an interview. 'My biggest disappointment was the cascade of Celtic scarves from the top deck of the Main Stand,' said Burns. 'That was a sadness for me but I can understand because it's built up over five years.'

After the final Burns took his players, including McStay, back to Celtic Park to face the club's supporters. His new chairman Fergus McCann had sat impassively throughout the disappointment.

'During the game Fergus McCann was up in the stand to our left and I remember at various points looking up at him,' says Richard Gordon. 'When Paul McStay missed his penalty I looked up and he was just stony-faced. There wasn't a flicker or a trace of emotion.'

McCann would later pledge that Celtic would go forward with their determination renewed. Burns would be in and out of the post-match press conference within 30 seconds. He spoke tersely, using just 23 words.

'I'll be very quick,' he said. 'I don't think anyone can imagine our disappointment. Cup finals are all about winners and it is Raith's day.'

Back on the pitch it was definitely Raith's day. Jason Rowbotham was grabbed by Chic Young and described the win as, 'a dream come true'. When the interviewer commented on his calm demeanour, he replied, 'I am taking it all in. I think I am still in shock.'

The rest of the players were still embracing each other in disbelief as they gathered for the presentation of the cup. Julian Broddle was next to express his incredulity at events to Young. 'I just can't believe what is happening here,' he said. 'We are now in Europe. It is unbelievable. For such a small club to do such a great thing as this, beating Celtic in such a superb stadium, it is just something else.'

The interviews were coming thick and fast and Ally Graham, resplendent in a Coca-Cola Cup baseball hat, began his own memorable interview with Young. 'I cannae believe it. I am going to burst into tears,' said Graham. 'This is absolutely unbelievable. I just cannae believe it.'

He reflects now on his interview, 'See when a guy grabs you right after a game, you don't know what to say. I just said it was unbelievable because that is exactly what it was.'

When Young asked him whether he was able to watch the shoot-out he continued, 'I was really, really nervous. I think I was next up and I didn't want to take a penalty so I prayed to God just for him to miss it.'

Sinclair contests Graham's claim that he was next up in the shoot-out.

'Big Ally Graham always said that he was next,' says Sinclair. 'But me and Ian Redford both said, "I'll go next" and I said to Ian, "OK, you go next, you're the experienced one" and he said to me, "No, you go next, you're the youngest." It was definitely me next but Thommo saved me the bother. You could not imagine the relief in my drawers at that moment.'

Ian Redford felt similarly relieved. 'As a teenage kid playing for Dundee, I would've grabbed the ball off anyone and stuck it in the back of the net without thinking,' said Redford. 'For some reason I just did not fancy this situation one little bit. As anyone who knows Paul will tell you, he is a very hard man to dislike or wish ill of, but at that moment I wanted him to miss that kick more than anything in the world.'

The players waited to collect the cup although the podium had been placed facing the now almost empty Main Stand at Ibrox. The Celtic support had vanished, leaving the stadium to supporters of the Kirkcaldy club.

'I looked around and the three stands were empty, apart from a few Celtic fans shouting abuse at their team,' says Tony Fimister. 'I couldn't believe that Ibrox could empty so quickly.'

A few small pockets of Celtic fans did remain to sportingly applaud the victors including some relatives of Sinclair. 'My family were among the few Celtic fans that stayed to see the cup presented,' he says. 'I ran to the Copland Road Stand where my uncles were and they were standing applauding me and giving me the two fingers at the same time.'

The Rovers support roared as the team started their walk to collect the cup. Captain Gordon Dalziel led the line and after kissing Penny Hughes from sponsors Coca-Cola, he was handed the cup. He planted another kiss on the trophy before raising it aloft with his left hand towards the Govan Stand. The Raith support roared their approval.

'The memory of the win over Celtic will be with me forever,' says Dalziel. 'I had won the League Cup with Rangers and played in the Scottish Cup Final but it was the greatest moment of my career to go up and lift the trophy. Being the captain it was a proud moment for me to go up and lift the cup for Raith Rovers. It was a terrific moment.'

The cup was passed along the line and as each player raised it to the crowd, the whole stand cheered. There was an especially exuberant cheer for Scott Thomson who had made the vital penalty save.

Young attempted to interview Nicholl for a second time and found him shaking but back in control of his emotions. He commiserated with McStay and Celtic before heaping praise on his players. Asked by Young where the win ranked in his successful career with Manchester United, Rangers and Northern Ireland, the Raith manager replied, 'There is absolutely no comparison.'

When Young evoked the memory of Sam Leith's infamous comment and asked whether they would be dancing in the streets of Raith tonight, Nicholl replied, 'Jigging, dancing, whatever you want to do, I'll be doing it!'

The players remained on the pitch to parade the cup in front of their supporters. Almost no one had left the Govan Stand as they wanted to savour the victory for as long as possible. Blue and white scarves were thrown down from the stands in the hope that they would adorn the victorious Raith players.

For John McStay, in the stand as a Rovers fan, the joy was tinged with a slight regret. 'I wished I was there,' he reflects. 'I had left in August that year and for the sake of what? I could have been there. It broke my heart to think I could have been part of that.'

When the celebrations subsided, the players headed towards the dressing room and the fans reluctantly drifted out of Ibrox. The mood in the dressing room was a mix of elation and stunned disbelief.

'By the time we eventually got in the changing room we had done so much celebrating outside on the field that it was pretty quiet,' says McAnespie. Many of the players were quietly contemplative as they tried to come to terms with what they had just achieved.

'It was the winding down time,' says Graham. 'Winding down and thinking, "We've done it!" A lot of us were just sitting by ourselves and trying to reflect on what we had just done. I watched it over again in my head just lying in the bath just to make sure we had done it.'

The subdued mood was shattered when the champagne arrived. 'After the game it was quite quiet for about five minutes,' recalls Thomson. 'Everybody was just sitting down trying to take it in. Boys were going around congratulating each other and all of a sudden the door opens and there is a wee case of champagne pushed in. Big Shaun said, "Come on," shakes up a bottle and it was bedlam after that.'

Julian Broddle describes the chaos. 'Everybody was jumping around and champagne was being chucked everywhere and Ally McCoist and Craig Brewster came running in,' he says. 'Ally was absolutely buzzing because he was such good friends with Jimmy Nic.'

McAnespie made sure that he secured a couple of mementos from the dressing-room party. 'They brought some boxes of Rangers' champagne in for us and I remember grabbing two bottles,' recalls the defender. 'I went back out of the changing room in my pads and my socks and went to the front door. The security guys were like, "Where are you going?" and I opened the front door and my parents were standing right there at the main door at Ibrox. My dad has still got two bottles and they have pride of place in the cabinet now.'

The Rovers players headed back to their bus for the journey back to Kirkcaldy. If any of the squad had not yet realised what they achieved then their departure from Ibrox reminded them.

'Coming out of Ibrox and getting on that bus with all the people in Govan hanging out their windows because we had beaten Celtic, all the Rangers brigade,' says Graham. 'That was a good memory. That brought it home that we had done it.'

'You got back on the team bus and John Valente was there,' says Stevie Crawford. 'The work that he did, it just showed what the club was about at the time. Players get all the credit but everybody played a massive part.'

The League Cup trophy sat proudly on the table that had been kept free on the journey to the final. It was to be a memorable journey back to Fife. 'We were passing bus after bus of Celtic supporters on the way back,' laughs Valente. 'The cup was there and I was saying, "Christ, put the light out!"'

One Rovers player who didn't make the return journey to Kirkcaldy was man of the match David Narey. He was content to forego the celebrations after the game as Gordon Dalziel explains. 'Narey was amazing during the game and unbelievable after it when he walked straight past the team bus that was headed for a spectacular night out in Kirkcaldy and got into his car,' he says.

'I'm told Davie went up the road and had a fish supper because that was his way.'

As the bus made its way back to Fife there was some singing, but many of the players sat quietly having put so much energy and emotion into the game.

The reception the team received when they reached Kirkcaldy was a shock. A large crowd had gathered at the Dean Park Hotel to greet their heroes on their return. 'Seeing the fans there was an amazing feeling,' says McAnespie. 'All those fans had been at the game and then they were there to see us coming back. We never expected anything like that coming back at all. We just thought we were heading back to Kirkcaldy and going to Jackie O's for the night.'

Although some fans had gathered at Stark's Park, the police ruled out a return to the stadium so the crowd made their way to the hotel. 'You couldn't even see the car park because of the number of people who were back there,' says Cameron.

It would be a night to remember for the players and the people of Kirkcaldy, although for some players recollections of the celebrations would become hazy as the alcohol flowed. 'The aftermath is pretty much a blur,' says Cameron. It was just a case of drink, drink and more drink. Any tiredness had gone, it was just pure adrenaline from what we had achieved and we were just going to make the most of it. We headed off down the High Street, although the directors didn't trust us with the cup!'

The Kirkcaldy public partied in the High Street and wanted to let the players know just how proud they were of their team. 'I could have gone anywhere in Kirkcaldy,' says Broddle. 'I had people saying to me, "Come into my house and have a beer," or, "You can stay here if you want."

'It was just a brilliant experience the few days after. I remember Jimmy telling us at the party back in Kirkcaldy, "Look, we have got a game at some point so I want you back by Wednesday." He said, "I don't care what you do from this point, but we need you back by Wednesday."'

There would be a civic reception later in the week but the next few days were about enjoying the moment. 'The next four or five days after were fantastic,' says Jason Dair. 'We were out and about in Kirkcaldy celebrating with the fans. There was also a civic reception I remember in the council building with the Lord Provost and lifting the trophy out on a balcony with all the fans in the street and surrounding area below. Most of the stories from that week can't be repeated.'

The party was to continue for a few days. 'We did a programme on the Tuesday or Wednesday night,' recalls Richard Gordon. 'Gordon Dalziel came in and he was still blitzed. I don't think he had slept. There was still almost that sense of disbelief that Rovers had beaten Celtic.'

There may still have been some disbelief, but it had happened. Raith Rovers had won their first national trophy.

19

WHAT A DAY THAT WAS
Stark's Park, Kirkcaldy, 28 November

JIMMY NICHOLL arrived at Stark's Park feeling rough. He had left the party in Kirkcaldy the previous evening and headed home to continue the celebrations in his home town.

'I went back to my local pub and I stopped drinking about 7.30am,' says Nicholl. 'I decided enough was enough and went to my bed only to be awoken by the phone at 10.30am. I was told I needed to be at Stark's Park for a press conference. I was still steaming and I remember I went there and I was an absolute mess both physically and mentally. I looked a right state but I couldn't have been happier.'

Goalkeeping hero Scott Thomson was also in demand from the media. 'The *Daily Record* had said to me, "Can we do a photograph with you Monday morning?"' says Thomson. '"I'll come to your room and we'll get a photograph of you sitting in your bed." I never went to my bed until five o'clock!'

There had been numerous other late nights in Kirkcaldy as the players and supporters celebrated their outrageous victory, yet the Kirkcaldy public was eager to awake the next day and read the newspaper accounts of the match.

The back pages of the newspapers were a delight for every Rovers supporter with the tabloid headline writers in overdrive. 'Rover the Moon'; 'Thank Gord'; 'Tic as a Parrot' and 'Scottcha', screamed *The Sun*. 'He's Scott it', 'It's Beyond Belief' and 'It's Rover and Out For Celts', proclaimed the *Daily Record*. 'It's Hip-Hip Hoo-Raith!' said the *Daily Mirror*.

Rodger Baillie of the *Daily Record* described the final poetically when he wrote, 'The soccer Cinderellas didn't just go to the ball...they stayed to claim the prize.' He added, 'Boss Jimmy Nicholl said last week he couldn't imagine AC Milan looking for training facilities at Burntisland. Well, the Italian giants and other big name European sides had better get their maps out.'

Graham Clark in *The Sun* described it as, 'A final that crackled, sparkled and fizzed like a lit firework's box from the first minute to the last.' The notoriously hard-to-please former Dundee United manager Jim McLean summed it up, 'A super final full of rugged competitiveness, goalmouth incidents galore and plenty of quality play from both sides.'

Every journalist was glowing in their praise for the Raith Rovers performance and the belief they had shown throughout the epic contest. There was no sense that the victory was undeserved.

Alex Cameron, writing in the *Record*, observed, 'Raith won as a team, Celtic lost as units.' *The Sun*'s Graham Clark agreed. 'Make no mistake,' he wrote, 'Raith deserved this first taste of cup glory. They took the lead, lost it, held their nerve as Celtic pounded them, forced a last-gasp equaliser, had the best of extra time and their stars kept their cool to sink six penalties.'

The victory was already being put forward as one of the greatest upsets in Scottish football history with Brian Scott of the *Record* describing it as, 'One of the most romantic chapters in the Scottish football legend.'

There was just one dissenting voice, with well-known curmudgeon Gerry McNee bemoaning the fact that the Kirkcaldy side was now in Europe. 'It is sheer madness that any team can gain a UEFA spot for winning the Coca-Cola Cup,' wrote McNee. 'A tournament I've said for years must be binned.' Any Rovers supporters reading his comments laughed them off as the bitter outpouring of a reporter whose Celtic sympathies were well known.

When the *Fife Free Press* was produced a few days later, John Greechan started his match report with the words, 'On a perfect Sunday afternoon in November 1994, the history books will from now on record, the Kirkcaldy club lifted their first major trophy since forming 111 years ago.' He went to on write, 'Beating the mighty Celtic in a national cup final has ensured that Jimmy Nicholl and his players will forever be immortalised in the hearts of the people of Kirkcaldy.'

Strangely, the paper's regular star check feature awarded most of the Raith players nine out of ten for the match, with only Scott Thomson and David Narey receiving the maximum score of ten. It begs the question, what sort of performance a Rovers team would have to put in for them all to score the maximum score of ten? Perhaps the local paper was deducting points for not having won the game over 90 minutes. It mattered not as to every Raith supporter the team would be legends forever and fondly remembered for their heroic efforts.

The historic match would be revisited in the first match programme after the win for a game against St Mirren on 6 December. The programme editor wrote, 'What remains to be said that has not already been said? Not a lot. Not much more than to reiterate just how important the victory is to a club like Raith Rovers. It is so much more than newly regained status; more than a prestigious trophy in the cabinet; more than a victory over one half of the Old Firm when it mattered most. It might just be the beginning of a whole new existence for our beloved club.

'We did it, and they were heroes to a man. And more to the point ten and a half thousand of us have the memories of being there. Supposing I never see another game as long as I live, I've seen my club make a dream a reality and for that I'm eternally grateful.'

His words summed up the emotions of every Raith fan who had been lucky enough to witness such a magnificent achievement. This was special and they knew it.

It was not just Rovers fans who recognised the uniqueness of what had happened. Broadcaster Richard Gordon believes it was one of the great finals. 'We are lucky to be at so many of these big events,' he says. 'UEFA Cup finals, Champions League finals, huge international matches but there is always something special when you are at a cup final and the underdog comes out on top.

'I found myself sucked into the whole thing. I was pleased for Jimmy Nicholl. Jimmy was a joy to work with. A lovely, lovely man and I was pleased he had taken Raith Rovers to a major trophy.'

Within a week, Rovers won another trophy as they were presented with the *Sportscene* Team of the Year award at a televised ceremony in Glasgow.

The League Cup win had an immediate impact on the Rovers squad and sparked them into life in their league title race. 'It was as if it was, "OK that's us. Let's go",' says Davie Sinclair. 'Like someone had just switched the lights on and we were winning every week. The buzz about the place was just incredible. We played Airdrie just after Christmas when every win was vital to catch the teams above us and I scored a last-minute winner. I couldn't believe I hit it so well. I haven't scored many goals in my career but there have been few better than that one.'

The victory over Airdrie sent Raith on an unbeaten run of 14 games in the First Division. 'Our season just snowballed,' says Colin Cameron. 'The aim was always to get back in the Premier Division. It was a massive confidence boost beating Celtic on that type of occasion so we just seemed to pick up speed in the league. After winning a cup it would have been easy for us to lose our way a wee bit but again such was the belief and character in the club that we went on an unbelievable run.'

The run took Rovers to the last league game of the season at Firhill where they secured the First Division title and a return to the top flight with a nervy 0-0 draw against Hamilton, becoming the first Raith Rovers team to win the 'double'. It had been a truly exceptional season.

'The players could quite easily have lived off the cup success and finished mid-table in the First Division but they really pushed themselves and deserved to win the title,' says Jimmy Nicholl. 'It just topped off the perfect season. From what we had built up in a short space of time, look what they had done – won the league and won a cup. It was brilliant.'

For one Raith player, that day at Firhill would prove to be the end of the line for his career in Kirkcaldy. Gordon Dalziel had been there at the start when Frank Connor began the rebuilding process that would lay the foundation for Nicholl and his squad to achieve their double victory. He was now club captain and had lifted the First Division trophy, months after lifting the League Cup. It was the perfect moment for Dalziel to end his love affair with the club.

'I remember sitting in the dressing room at Firhill and thinking, "This is the last game I will ever play for Raith Rovers",' says Dalziel. 'I knew that from where we had come from, winning the cup, winning the league, being the captain, and every year I was there I was top goalscorer. I knew that I had got to where I wanted to go.

'It was like climbing a mountain. You get to the top and you think, "That is it for me now." It was a great way to leave the club. We went on a journey and it ended at Firhill at quarter to five. What a fantastic journey.'

It had indeed been a fantastic journey for everyone associated with the Kirkcaldy club. They had travelled from the depths of the Second Division to winning the League Cup in less than a decade.

'It is up there as one of the great moments in modern day Scottish football history,' says Richard Gordon. 'To come from where they were and achieve what they did in such a short space of time and all the while bringing through a group of young players. For most of us, these moments come along and sustain you for evermore. They are to be cherished and treasured.'

Even the player who suffered the pain of missing the vital penalty is fulsome in his praise of the Raith Rovers team he encountered. There is no hint of bitterness as he recalls the achievements of the Kirkcaldy side.

'As a team Raith played with a confident carefree attitude, in particular the younger players,' says Paul McStay. 'Raith had some high quality younger players on their books with Colin Cameron, Stevie Crawford, Jason Dair and Steve McAnespie. It was no surprise that Raith were promoted at the end of that season and had a great journey into Europe when they came up against Bayern Munich.

'To win cups and to be able to compete against the best in Europe you need a team with quality players, the tactical know-how and the will to win. Raith Rovers definitely had it.'

The manager who started it all off agrees. 'Raith Rovers never got it easy,' says Frank Connor. 'You were entitled to be proud because you earned it. Nobody gave you it. Nine years from where the club was to winning the cup. That wasn't bad was it? To be honest with you, that is a story to be told in football. You can't get any better than that.'

There were many people who helped play a part, large or small, in that remarkable success but most cherished among them are the players and management team who were at Ibrox Stadium on that clear November day at Ibrox in 1994 for the greatest day in Raith Rovers' history. It was a time in their lives that they would never forget.

'When I was a youngster I thought the ultimate was scoring in an Old Firm game, which I did, but now looking back, to help Raith Rovers to win a major competition against Celtic is the highlight,' says Dalziel.

'I have had some great times in football but Raith Rovers will always be the biggest part of my football life, not just for the football but for the people I still call friends in Kirkcaldy and the players I was privileged to play alongside and for the managers I played under and who I regard as great, great friends of mine now. It was a special time. I don't think it will ever be bettered.'

Nicholl feels the same. 'Those were six of the happiest years of my life,' he says. 'What a journey I had at Raith Rovers. I went all the way from having only a handful of full-time players to a League Cup win. It was a great collection of everything: good dressing room, good players, good professionals, good staff; great scouts, Gerry Docherty the physio, Jackie, John Brown; everything was spot on. It was just muck and nettles and it just worked. They were great, great times.

'There are three games that mean the most to me in my career: Northern Ireland beating Spain 1-0 when we were down to ten men; Man United beating Liverpool to win the cup when Liverpool were favourites for the treble and then Raith Rovers beating Celtic. In every game we were massive underdogs and these results show you how fantastic the game of football can be.'

Englishman Julian Broddle feels privileged to have been a part of it and now considers a small corner of Scotland 'home'. 'When I go up there, it just feels like I am in the right place and it is where I should be,' he says. 'Great memories but good, good friends I can always rely on, probably for the rest of my life.

'Whenever I go up there and meet up with them it's not a case of, "How are you doing? Are you alright?" The piss-taking starts again right away. It is as if you'd seen each other last week. It was not like all the top players who go to cup finals and win championships regularly, it was so special for us and for Raith and for Kirkcaldy. They were amazing times and I wish we could do them all again.'

For many of the players the League Cup win was the highlight of their careers. 'Without question it was the best feeling I've ever had in my life and I'd love to go back and relive it,' says Ally Graham. 'For a club like Raith Rovers to do that was a dream come true. There is no doubt about that. It is amazing what we did.'

Davie Sinclair sums up the thoughts of many of his fellow players when he says succinctly, 'It was the best day of my life.'

Even Cameron, who would go on to achieve considerable success with Hearts, Wolves and Scotland, believes that his time at Raith was extra special. 'Raith beating Celtic has probably got to be credited as the best thing I have achieved in my career and I have been very fortunate,' says Cameron.

'The cup finals and play-off wins were all special but I would still say that it was the best one because we were a First Division club playing one of the best teams in the country and we beat them. We just met things head-on and didn't feel sorry for ourselves. We just kept at it, kept at it and kept the belief.'

It was that fighting spirit and belief throughout the cup run and in the final which most sticks out for Stephen McAnespie. 'I think we were battle-scarred from the previous rounds and what we had had to go through,' says McAnespie. 'We knew how to fight and we knew how to stay in the fight and come back from adversity and overcome things. A lot of teams go up against the Old Firm now and suddenly they collapse. The moment overawes them. Jimmy had us in a mindset where we could beat anybody at the time. We were a bunch of young guys who were not scared to play against anyone. We were fearless.

'We were such a good group of guys. We came from nowhere; just a bunch of working-class boys who were fighting for each other. A wee team from Kirkcaldy doing something that big! I have won things afterwards, getting promotion and stuff like that but none of that compares to what we did that year.'

Goalkeeper Brian Potter feels privileged to have played a role in such a significant achievement. 'We just had a belief and a lot of that came from Jimmy,' says Potter. 'It is coming on 20 years ago but people still come up and talk to me about it. It was the best time I had in football. Every time I go back into Stark's Park you just look at the photos and it just brings it all back to you. You think about that time and it was just unbelievable to be about the club at the time. I was lucky to be there and fortunate to play a wee bit of a part in it.'

Throughout all the interviews with the players who helped Raith Rovers achieve their success over that period the one word that features most regularly is 'togetherness'. The bonds between the players, between the management and the players and between the players and the supporters, were some of the strongest many had experienced in football.

'I recall coming back on the team bus after we won the championship against Hamilton at Firhill, and having a long chat with Julian Broddle,' says Scott Thomson. 'He mentioned that he had been in the game for a lot of years, starting in first-team football at 16 and he had never known a team spirit like we had at the Rovers. We had a set of players who would give blood, sweat and tears for you and a good manager who ran it brilliantly.'

For many, lifelong friendships were forged in the Stark's Park dressing room. 'I'm still very close to a few of the boys from then which is great,' says Jason Dair. 'Every few years, when it's an anniversary or there is a function that gets everyone back together, it's always good.'

Jason Rowbotham agrees. 'I look back on my time with Raith Rovers with great affection,' he says. 'Not only because of the trophies we won but because of the friends I made.'

Striker Stevie Crawford believes it was a special time at a special club. 'When you speak about that period in Raith Rovers' history it puts a smile on people's faces,' he says. 'Looking back at the success and the dressing room we had, I would say it was the greatest spell in my playing career. Mention Raith Rovers and every person at the club meant something: Jock Brown, Jackie, Andy Leigh, Susan and Kerry in the office, Mr Campsie, Dennis O'Connell, Jim O'Connell, supporters – the names go over the years but you remember faces – I was fortunate that I was part of that and am proud to be part of that.

'I hope that as a coach I can bring something of what I was given at Raith Rovers: the work put in to be a good team-mate, to grow up from being a boy to being a man, being able to conduct myself in the right manner, win, lose or draw and treat people within a club who have a love for the game the same way Jimmy did. If I can give someone even a fraction of what Raith Rovers gave me, then I will be happy. That warmness, that togetherness, to be lucky enough to have been part of that will live with me to the day I die.'

Crawford reflects the thoughts of every Raith Rovers fan who was lucky enough to be part of that glorious period in the club's history.

Being a Raith fan, like being a fan of most of Scotland's provincial clubs, isn't easy. There isn't the regular diet of success and dominance that accompanies the easy option of following the Old Firm. There is disappointment, disenchantment and periods of downright farce when the club doesn't deserve our attention, never mind our unswerving loyalty. There are cold nights in Stranraer, humiliating defeats in Kirkcaldy and times when we feel like abandoning our football club to allow it to hurt us no further.

There will be defeats and disappointment in the future which will test our loyalty and erode our affection. We are not unique. The generations of supporters before us, who may have passed down their love of Raith Rovers to us, witnessed considerable effort and toil but little success. The generations to come, perhaps even our own descendants, will also learn to love Raith Rovers and embrace the frustration and disappointment that accompanies it.

But we will all have one glorious moment in the history of our club in common. The moment when a team of players, young and old, experienced and inexperienced, from Scotland, England and Wales and managed by a likeable Northern Irishman, travelled to Glasgow on a cold November afternoon and defied the odds to take the cup back to Kirkcaldy.

The date of 27 November 1994 is one that will live on in the history of Raith Rovers forever and for those of us who were lucky enough to have witnessed it, it's a moment that will stay with us forever. It is part of our memory, part of our lives and part of us. It may have been unthinkable, but it happened and we were there to see it.

Epilogue

DREAMS NEVER END

Stark's Park, Kirkcaldy, 27 March 2011

PAUL McSTAY walked forward to take his penalty. He shook hands with his cousin John on the way. The Raith Rovers supporters in the South Stand clapped him as he made his approach. As he began his run-up, the Rovers crowd raised the noise levels to put him off.

He displayed none of the nervousness of his penalty 16 years earlier and sent the ball cleanly into the net past Scott Thomson. His goal was greeted with boos but they quickly dissipated into applause for the former Celtic captain. There was appreciation from the Raith support that McStay had travelled from his home in Australia to help re-create the 1994 League Cup Final in a benefit match for Rovers player Ronnie Coyle.

Although he didn't feature in the League Cup Final due to injury, Ronnie epitomises the spirit of the journey Rovers made between 1985 and 1994. He had started his football career with Celtic Boys' Club when he signed an S-form at the age of 14. He progressed through the reserves and into the first team aged 19, under the management of Billy McNeill.

A number of other clubs expressed an interest in the young Ronnie including Manchester United and Dundee United but having been brought up with the Celtic tradition he remained committed to the Parkhead club. The arrival of Davie Hay as manager was to signal the beginning of the end of Ronnie's time at Celtic.

'Davie Hay came in and that's when things started to go wrong,' said Ronnie. 'There were a lot of injuries and I was brought into the first team against Dundee United and we lost 4-2. I was left out the following week against Aberdeen and from then on the writing was on the wall.'

He eventually moved to England where he played for first Middlesbrough then Rochdale. It was during Ronnie's spell with Rochdale that Frank Connor approached him to help him rebuild Raith Rovers.

'Frank has been different class to me throughout the whole of my career,' said Ronnie. 'He took a lot of interest in me at Celtic, where we had a reserve team that went two seasons unbeaten. We had a special relationship and he brought me to Raith, and the main factor in me deciding to come was Frank was there. Frank organised a full-time job for me in financial services through a friend, because the Rovers were part-time.'

Like most players who joined during the Connor era there was an initial sense of concern about arriving in Kirkcaldy from Ronnie. 'On my first night there, it was kind of bleak,' he says. 'It was part-time, there were precious few training facilities and you took your kit home to wash it. I thought, "What the hell am I doing?"'

Ronnie would go on to become a regular feature in the Raith Rovers line-up as they progressed through the divisions.

Team-mate Gordon Dalziel recalls the character of the defender. 'He was a really, really decent bloke,' says Dalziel. 'He liked his arguments, he liked his debates, he liked his wee fall-outs just like the rest of us, but a great guy, a great footballer and a great competitor.'

Ronnie was a popular figure in the Rovers dressing room even if he tended to be on the receiving end of a lot of abuse from his fellow players.

'He was probably the father figure of the team,' says Colin Cameron. 'He got absolute dog's abuse from us young ones because of the type of person that he was. It was so funny because he could never catch any of the young lads and that made us give him more abuse. But he always took it the right way. He was probably one of the biggest influences in the club.'

Craig Brewster recalls his friend's competitive spirit, 'He was one of the traditional, playing centre-halves but one day I wound him up so much in training that he just volleyed me off the ball, booting me up the arse, warning me not to do that again. So he was tough as well.

'When we played St Mirren in the first game of the season after they had just been relegated, we beat them 7-0, but he scored the third goal and it was the only one that mattered! It was a peach, and Ronnie dribbled the length of the pitch before slotting it home. He said it was Baresi-like. He thought he was Baresi! He wasn't, but he was a wonderful man.'

One of the highlights of Ronnie's career was playing in the UEFA Cup with Raith in the ties against Gotu Ittrotarfelag from the Faroe Islands, IA Akranes from Iceland and the German giants Bayern Munich. Coyle was part of the team that famously led Bayern 1-0 at half-time from a deflected Danny Lennon free kick. Coyle's slip in the second half effectively ended Rovers' hopes in the tie and he recalled it years later.

'The ball came down to the bottom corner, big Shaun shouted to me that I had time, I took a touch and fell on my arse,' he said. 'The German was on the ball in a flash and it was 1-1. None of the players blamed me but at the time I blamed myself, which was probably one of the worst things I could do.

'At the end of the day you can't legislate for bad luck and that's all it was. It wasn't as if I tried to beat somebody with skill and made a mess of it. I had long studs in, the pitch was wet, and I fell on my arse.' He added, laughing, 'I'm going to blame Shaun Dennis. He shouted, "Time!"'

Cameron recalls comforting Ronnie after the match. 'When we all came back into the dressing room at the end of that match we could see it was playing on his mind,' says Cameron. 'So we all made a point of going over to him and telling him we didn't blame him in any way, and it says a lot about him that he was quite humbled by that. He did beat himself up about it. He was the type of guy that would take everything on his shoulders; he was a lovely guy.'

Ronnie left Rovers and had spells as a player at Ayr United, Albion Rovers, East Fife and then Queen's Park. He hung up his boots in 1999.

The nine years that Ronnie spent in Kirkcaldy had left an indelible mark on him. When the club were struggling financially and looking to free themselves from bad ownership in the summer of 2005, he was quick to offer his support to the Reclaim the Rovers campaign. His willingness to help out and offer support was reciprocated when he was first diagnosed with an acute form of leukaemia in March 2009.

Raith supporters sent messages of support and well wishes to their former player as he struggled to cope with the disease. A bone marrow transplant seven months later gave him hope and he had recovered enough to make a return to Stark's Park for a half-time appearance in a match against Ross County. He was greeted by a spontaneous standing ovation by the Rovers fans and the crowd chanted his name for so long that he was overcome with emotion and could barely speak.

Ronnie would later say, 'I didn't expect to end up greetin' like a big lassie but I never thought that somebody could be given a welcome like that. I was asked to say a few words but I couldn't even speak. It was special, really special.'

After the game, Ronnie thanked the fans in an interview for the Rovers website. 'Thank you,' he said. 'The support has been overwhelming. The good wishes and everything else that has come from the Rovers family has just been fantastic,' before joking that the reception he had received was, 'not bad for a Weegie'.

Ronnie went on to reflect on his time at the club. 'Nine years at one club is a long time,' he said. 'It is something that I am proud of. I am proud of where we started with the club and where we ended up finishing with the club. What we achieved as a small, provincial club was phenomenal. It is just one of those clubs. It never leaves you.

'We played as a family, we suffered as a family and even in the really bad times the family support was there for me through my darkest year.'

When he received news that the cancer had returned it was a devastating blow for Ronnie and his family and friends. He underwent another dose of chemotherapy. As Ronnie battled the disease for a second time, the idea of a benefit match was formed.

'I was sitting on a building site one day and I phoned Denis O'Connell's brother, Jim,' recalls Davie Sinclair. 'I said, "I think we should have a match for Ronnie. The teams of 94/95 should get together." Jim said he thought it was a fantastic idea.'

The match was soon organised with a lot of hard work and effort from Ronnie's closest friends and supporters. Fittingly, Raith Rovers and Celtic drew again in front of almost 3,000 fans and McStay's penalty helped the Glasgow team to victory, perhaps exorcising some demons of the past.

The former Scotland star explains how he made sure that he scored. 'Obviously the match ended in a draw, an exciting 3-3 tie and you know what that meant, it had to go to penalties!' says McStay. 'So it was set up for the keeper to save my penalty again so I indicated to him, "Yip same way." So he went the same way as 94 and I slotted it home the other way. At least it gave Ronnie a wee giggle!'

McStay recalls how he first met the young Ronnie. 'Our recollections of when we first met are slightly different but I would say my version is 100 per cent. I really couldn't forget the day as it was my first game in the Hoops. I was invited in to play for Celtic Boys' Club in a friendly match. I was recalling this wonderful memory to Ronnie but he says that he doesn't remember me from that day and that I must have played crap. He says we met the following year at Celtic training!'

The two young footballers would become close friends as they trained together on the red ash pitch at Celtic's training ground at Barrowfield.

'Ronnie was a dedicated young player that had the desire to make the grade,' recalls McStay. 'He worked very hard at his game. Our friendship grew through our training at Celtic and the wonderful journey that we both had in the Scottish national teams. We had a good few years in the set-up together with the pinnacle being the Scottish Schoolboys under-15s' win over England at Wembley when we hammered them 5-4.

'It was a very memorable game which still gets mentioned after all these years which is quite remarkable for a schoolboy match. It was a deft touch through by Ronnie that set up my first goal that day and, as he reminded me on a couple of occasions, "He made me".'

McStay recalls the ability and commitment of his friend. 'Ronnie had very good technique and passing ability but above all he was a great defender, if a little bit aggressive at times!' he says. 'I often felt the brunt of Ronnie's will to win and commitment during matches against Raith and even in training when he was my team-mate at Celtic. I can still see very clearly the night at Celtic Park when he took out John Collins and me in one tackle!'

Ronnie's competitive attitude would manifest itself off the pitch as well as on. No matter what Ronnie did, he wanted to win.

'He had the will to win in his character,' says McStay. 'That not only came out on the park but during our marathon snooker sessions and jaunts on to the golf course. Ronnie was a very good golfer and he had the upper hand there, although on occasions his three iron travelled further than his golf ball! But on the green baize I think I had him.'

When asked to appear at the benefit match, McStay had no hesitation in agreeing. 'The 94 final created the backdrop to a very emotional and fitting tribute to Ronnie,' says McStay. 'There were eight players from our 1994 cup final team that played in the match along with friends from Ronnie's playing days including my brothers Willie and Raymond. There were some wisecracks about penalties but the day was fun and hopefully we managed to entertain the fans and put on a decent show for Ronnie.'

After the match, players and fans attended a dinner to honour Ronnie and what he had achieved throughout his career. During the auction to help raise funds for Ronnie and his family one guest bid on the League Cup Final medal that Davie Kirkwood had generously donated. When the winning bidder collected the medal, he simply handed it back to the former Rovers midfielder. It was an act of generosity that summed up the friendship and togetherness that defined the day.

'It is a day that Joan, Kevin, Briony and Georgia along with Ronnie's family and friends will cherish,' says McStay. 'It was a magnificent day and I know Ronnie was very appreciative and humbled by the response from everyone that attended the match and the function. For me it was what he deserved, recognition and validation from the football community for his excellent career and for being such a wonderful person.'

'It was a fantastic day,' says Sinclair. 'A sad day but a fantastic day and he loved it. He was just sitting talking to everybody. None of us wanted it to end. He was one of the nicest guys you could ever meet.'

Brewster agrees. 'The whole day was an enormous credit to the man,' says Brewster. 'Paul McStay came all the way over from Australia to play. What more can you say? It was just a fantastic day. The support we had was incredible. I'll never forget when we scored the goal at the home support end. The roar brought back memories of when it was full and rocking.

'That day meant so much to him and to us all. He was still up at 4am, he didn't want to miss a thing. I don't think any of us wanted it to end.'

For many of the Rovers players it rekindled memories of their successful period in the late 1980s and 90s and the bonds they had as a squad.

'The dressing room was exactly the same,' says Gordon Dalziel. 'I think it was Gary Pallister that turned around and said, "Jesus Christ, I've never been in a dressing room like this before," because it was just the same.'

Stevie Crawford laughs as he recalls the atmosphere before and after the game. 'Nothing was different,' he says. 'Daz was having a laugh and everyone was having a laugh in the dressing room before the game. We were just older, uglier and fatter but it was just like turning the clock back. I know that everybody goes here, there and everywhere in their life but all the boys got the team photo from that day, we all got one and it goes back to what we thought of Raith Rovers at the time.

'Coylie didn't want you to be sad on the day of the game. He wanted the boys to have a pint and enjoy the evening. He was focused on that. It wasn't a night to feel sorry for him. I was sitting with him and I can always remember Coylie saying to me personally that the hardest thing was not what was going to happen, but what he was leaving behind.'

Ronnie later expressed his gratitude to all who had helped make the day possible. 'The day itself could not have gone any better,' he said. 'The people of Kirkcaldy turned out to show their friendship for me and I was delighted at how things went. There was a great turnout and it was good to see a lot of old friends. Getting the opportunity to speak with Gordon Brown was quite special. He took the time to bring his two kids along and was really nice and very down to earth.'

He singled out his friend and former Celtic team-mate McStay for special praise, 'Paul came a long way from Australia for the game and to make that effort was just tremendous. He put away his penalty well, which probably put to bed a few bad memories for him. It was fantastic to see him stick the ball away. It was great to have all my mates and my family there by my side. It was a special day.'

Just 16 days later Ronnie passed away suddenly and painlessly in a Glasgow hospital. He was aged 46 and left behind his wife Joan, and children Kevin, Briony and Georgia.

Ally Gourlay, chairman of the Raith Rovers Former Players Association, expressed the feelings of every Rovers supporter when he said that the club had lost a true friend.

Reflecting on the loss of his team-mate and friend, Colin Cameron says, 'I'm just glad we all got together with him at the benefit match and had a chance to have a laugh and talk about old times. Those are more memories we will treasure. He will never be forgotten.'

The former Rovers midfielder is correct. Ronnie Coyle will never be forgotten, and neither will his team-mates who helped Raith Rovers make the journey from the depths of the Second Division to that November day at Ibrox in 1994. They have all earned their place in the history of this proud club from Kirkcaldy. They will forever have a place in the hearts of every Raith Rovers fan, both now and in the future, as the players who defied the odds and achieved the unthinkable.

LEAGUE TABLES 1985–1995

Scottish Second Division 1985/86

		P	W	D	L	GF	GA	GD	Pts
1	Dunfermline Athletic (C)	39	23	11	5	91	47	44	57
2	Queen of the South (P)	39	23	9	7	71	36	35	55
3	Meadowbank Thistle	39	19	11	9	68	45	23	49
4	Queen's Park	39	19	8	12	61	39	22	46
5	Stirling Albion	39	18	8	13	57	53	4	44
6	St Johnstone	39	18	6	15	63	55	8	42
7	Stenhousemuir	39	16	8	15	55	63	-8	40
8	Arbroath	39	15	9	15	56	50	6	39
9	**Raith Rovers**	**39**	**15**	**7**	**17**	**67**	**65**	**2**	**37**
10	Cowdenbeath	39	14	9	16	52	53	-1	37
11	East Stirlingshire	39	11	6	22	49	69	-20	28
12	Berwick Rangers	39	7	11	21	45	80	-35	25
13	Albion Rovers	39	8	8	23	38	86	-48	24
14	Stranraer	39	9	5	25	41	83	-42	23

Scottish Second Division 1986/87

		P	W	D	L	GF	GA	GD	Pts
1	Meadowbank Thistle (C)	39	23	9	7	69	38	31	55
2	**Raith Rovers (P)**	**39**	**16**	**20**	**3**	**73**	**44**	**29**	**52**
3	Stirling Albion	39	20	12	7	55	33	22	52
4	Ayr United	39	22	8	9	70	49	21	52
5	St Johnstone	39	16	13	10	59	49	10	45
6	Alloa Athletic	39	17	7	15	48	50	-2	41
7	Cowdenbeath	39	16	8	15	59	55	4	40
8	Albion Rovers	39	15	9	15	48	51	-3	39
9	Queen's Park	39	9	19	11	48	49	-1	37
10	Stranraer	39	9	11	19	41	59	-18	29
11	Arbroath	39	11	7	21	46	66	-20	29
12	Stenhousemuir	39	10	9	20	37	58	-21	29
13	East Stirlingshire	39	6	11	22	33	56	-23	23
14	Berwick Rangers	39	8	7	24	40	69	-29	23

Scottish First Division 1987/88

		P	W	D	L	GF	GA	GD	Pts
1	Hamilton Accies (C)	44	22	12	10	67	39	28	56
2	Meadowbank Thistle	44	20	12	12	70	51	19	52
3	Clydebank	44	21	7	16	59	61	-2	49
4	Forfar Athletic	44	16	16	12	67	58	9	48
5	**Raith Rovers**	**44**	**19**	**7**	**18**	**81**	**76**	**5**	**45**
6	Airdrieonians	44	16	13	15	65	68	-3	45
7	Queen of the South	44	14	15	15	56	67	-11	43
8	Partick Thistle	44	16	9	19	60	64	-4	41
9	Clyde	44	17	6	21	73	75	-2	40
10	Kilmarnock	44	13	11	20	55	60	-5	37
11	East Fife (R)	44	13	10	21	61	76	-15	36
12	Dumbarton (R)	44	12	12	20	51	70	-19	36

Scottish First Division 1988/89

		P	W	D	L	GF	GA	GD	Pts
1	Dunfermline Athletic (C)	39	22	10	7	60	36	24	54
2	Falkirk	39	22	8	9	71	37	34	52
3	Clydebank	39	18	12	9	80	55	25	48
4	Airdrieonians	39	17	13	9	66	44	22	47
5	Morton	39	16	9	14	46	46	0	41
6	St Johnstone	39	14	12	13	51	42	9	40
7	**Raith Rovers**	**39**	**15**	**10**	**14**	**50**	**52**	**-2**	**40**
8	Partick Thistle	39	13	11	15	57	58	-1	37
9	Forfar Athletic	39	10	16	13	52	56	-4	36
10	Meadowbank Thistle	39	13	10	16	45	50	-5	36
11	Ayr United	39	13	9	17	56	72	-16	35
12	Clyde	39	9	16	14	40	52	-12	34
13	Kilmarnock (R)	39	10	14	15	47	60	-13	34
14	Queen of the South (R)	39	2	8	29	38	99	-61	12

Scottish First Division 1989/90

		P	W	D	L	GF	GA	GD	Pts
1	St Johnstone (C)	39	25	8	6	81	39	42	58
2	Airdrieonians	39	23	8	8	77	45	32	54
3	Clydebank	39	17	10	12	74	64	10	44
4	Falkirk	39	14	15	10	59	46	13	43
5	**Raith Rovers**	**39**	**15**	**12**	**12**	**57**	**50**	**7**	**42**
6	Hamilton Accies	39	14	13	12	52	53	-1	41
7	Meadowbank Thistle	39	13	13	13	41	46	-5	39
8	Partick Thistle	39	12	14	13	62	53	9	38
9	Clyde	39	10	15	14	39	46	-7	35
10	Ayr United	39	11	13	15	41	62	-21	35
11	Morton	39	9	16	14	38	46	-8	34
12	Forfar Athletic	39	8	15	16	51	65	-14	29
13	Albion Rovers (R)	39	8	11	20	50	78	-28	27
14	Alloa Athletic (R)	39	6	13	20	41	70	-29	25

Scottish First Division 1990/91

		P	W	D	L	GF	GA	GD	Pts
1	Falkirk (C)	39	21	12	6	70	35	35	54
2	Airdrieonians (P)	39	21	11	7	69	43	26	53
3	Dundee	39	22	8	9	59	33	26	52
4	Partick Thistle	39	16	13	10	56	53	3	45
5	Kilmarnock	39	15	13	11	58	48	10	43
6	Hamilton Accies	39	16	10	13	50	41	9	42
7	**Raith Rovers**	**39**	**14**	**9**	**16**	**54**	**64**	**-10**	**37**
8	Clydebank	39	13	10	16	65	70	-5	36
9	Morton	39	11	13	15	48	55	-7	35
10	Forfar Athletic	39	9	15	15	50	57	-7	33
11	Meadowbank Thistle	39	10	13	16	56	68	-12	33
12	Ayr United	39	10	12	17	47	59	-12	32
13	Clyde (R)	39	9	9	21	41	61	-20	27
14	Brechin City (R)	39	7	10	22	44	80	-36	24

Scottish First Division 1991/92

		P	W	D	L	GF	GA	GD	Pts
1	Dundee (C)	44	23	12	9	80	48	32	58
2	Partick Thistle (P)	44	23	11	10	62	36	26	57
3	Hamilton Accies	44	22	13	9	72	48	24	57
4	Kilmarnock	44	21	12	11	59	37	22	54
5	**Raith Rovers**	**44**	**21**	**11**	**12**	**59**	**42**	**17**	**53**
6	Ayr United	44	18	11	15	63	55	8	47
7	Morton	44	17	12	15	66	59	7	46
8	Stirling Albion	44	14	13	17	50	57	-7	41
9	Clydebank	44	12	12	20	59	77	-18	36
10	Meadowbank Thistle	44	7	16	21	37	59	-22	30
11	Montrose (R)	44	5	17	22	45	85	-40	27
12	Forfar Athletic (R)	44	5	12	27	36	85	-49	22

Scottish First Division 1992/93

		P	W	D	L	GF	GA	GD	Pts
1	**Raith Rovers** (C)	**44**	**25**	**15**	**4**	**85**	**41**	**44**	**65**
2	Kilmarnock (P)	44	21	12	11	67	40	27	54
3	Dunfermline Athletic	44	22	8	14	64	47	17	52
4	St Mirren	44	21	9	14	62	52	10	51
5	Hamilton Accies	44	19	12	13	65	45	20	50
6	Morton	44	19	10	15	65	56	9	48
7	Ayr United	44	14	18	12	49	44	5	46
8	Clydebank	44	16	13	15	71	66	5	45
9	Dumbarton	44	15	7	22	56	71	-15	37
10	Stirling Albion	44	11	13	20	44	61	-17	35
11	Meadowbank Thistle (R)	44	11	10	23	51	80	-29	32
12	Cowdenbeath (R)	44	3	7	34	33	109	-76	13

Scottish Premier Division 1993/94

		P	W	D	L	GF	GA	GD	Pts
1	Rangers (C)	44	22	14	8	74	41	33	58
2	Aberdeen	44	17	21	6	58	36	22	55
3	Motherwell	44	20	14	10	58	43	15	54
4	Celtic	44	15	20	9	51	38	13	50
5	Hibernian	44	16	15	13	53	48	5	47
6	Dundee United	44	11	20	13	47	48	-1	42
7	Heart of Midlothian	44	11	20	13	37	43	-6	42
8	Kilmarnock	44	12	16	16	36	45	-9	40
9	Partick Thistle	44	12	16	16	46	57	-11	40
10	St Johnstone (R)	44	10	20	14	35	47	-12	40
11	**Raith Rovers (R)**	**44**	**6**	**19**	**19**	**46**	**80**	**-34**	**31**
12	Dundee	44	8	13	23	42	57	-15	29

Scottish First Division 1994/95

		P	W	D	L	GF	GA	GD	Pts
1	**Raith Rovers (C)**	**36**	**19**	**12**	**5**	**54**	**32**	**22**	**69**
2	Dunfermline Athletic	36	18	14	4	73	37	36	68
3	Dundee	36	20	8	8	65	36	29	68
4	Airdrieonians	36	17	10	9	50	33	17	61
5	St Johnstone	36	14	14	8	59	39	20	56
6	Hamilton Accies	36	14	7	15	42	48	-6	49
7	St Mirren	36	8	12	16	34	50	-16	36
8	Clydebank	36	8	11	17	33	47	-14	35
9	Ayr United (R)	36	6	11	19	31	58	-27	29
10	Stranraer (R)	36	4	5	27	25	81	-56	17

MEMORABLE MATCHES

9 May 1987
Second Division

Stranraer 1 Raith Rovers 4

Stair Park, Stranraer
Attendance: 625
Goals: Creany (4); Dalziel (32, 49), Marshall (51), Harris (52)

 1 McAlpine
 2 Herd
 3 Sweeney
 4 Robertson
 5 Brash
 6 Kerr
 7 Simpson
 8 Marshall
 9 Harris
10 Gordon
11 Dalziel
Subs: Harrow (unused), Purdie (unused)

8 February 1988
Scottish Cup third round

Raith Rovers 0 Rangers 0

Stark's Park, Kirkcaldy
Attendance: 9,500

1 McAlpine
2 McStay
3 Harrow
4 Fraser
5 Brash
6 Gibson
7 Simpson
8 Coyle
9 Harris
10 Dalziel
11 Sweeney

Subs: Lloyd (for Dalziel, 64), Marshall (unused)

28 January 1989
Scottish Cup third round

Raith Rovers 1 Rangers 1

Stark's Park, Kirkcaldy
Attendance: 9,422
Goals: Dalziel (53); I. Ferguson (67)

1 Arthur
2 McStay
3 Murray
4 Fraser
5 Glennie
6 Gibson
7 Ferguson, I
8 Dalziel
9 Logan
10 Coyle
11 Sweeney

Subs: Marshall (for Dalziel, 73), Romaines (for Logan, 79)

10 April 1993
First Division

Raith Rovers 2 Dumbarton 0

Stark's Park, Kirkcaldy
Attendance: 4,893
Goals: Brewster (27, 48)

1 Arthur
2 McStay
3 McLeod
4 Coyle
5 Dennis
6 Raeside
7 Nicholl
8 Dalziel
9 Hetherston
10 Brewster
11 Cameron
Subs: Crawford (for McStay, 65), Dair (for Dalziel, 71)

17 August 1994
League Cup second round

Ross County 0 Raith Rovers 5

Victoria Park, Dingwall
Attendance: 2,288
Goals: Graham (65, 83, 88), Cameron (55), Dalziel (74)

1 Thomson
2 Rowbotham
3 Kirkwood
4 Coyle
5 Raeside
6 Sinclair
7 Lennon
8 Dalziel
9 Graham
10 Cameron
11 Dair
Subs: Broddle (unused), Crawford (unused), Potter (unused)

31 August 1994
League Cup third round

Raith Rovers 3 Kilmarnock 2

Stark's Park, Kirkcaldy
Attendance: 4,181
Goals: Cameron (35, 41, 77); Montgomerie (33), Williamson (79)

1 Thomson
2 McAnespie
3 Broddle
4 Rowbotham
5 Narey
6 Sinclair
7 Lennon
8 Dalziel
9 Graham
10 Cameron
11 Redford
Subs: Crawford (for Dalziel, 69), Coyle (for Redford, 81), Potter (unused)

20 September 1994
League Cup quarter-final

St Johnstone 1 Raith Rovers 3

McDiarmid Park, Perth
Attendance: 6,287
Goals: O'Neill (50); Dennis (19), Graham (29), Lennon (83)

1 Thomson
2 McAnespie
3 Broddle
4 Rowbotham
5 Dennis
6 Sinclair
7 Nicholl
8 Crawford
9 Graham
10 Cameron
11 Lennon
Subs: Dair (for Crawford, 81), Redford (unused), Potter (unused)

25 October 1994
League Cup semi-final

Raith Rovers 1 Airdrie 1 AET
(Raith Rovers won 5-4 on penalties)
McDiarmid Park, Perth
Attendance: 7,260
Goals: Graham (39); Cooper (74)

  1 Thomson (sent off 69)
  2 McAnespie
  3 Broddle
  4 Sinclair
  5 Dennis
  6 Narey
  7 Lennon
  8 Dalziel
  9 Graham
10 Cameron
11 Kirkwood
Subs: Crawford (for Dalziel, 51), Potter (for Kirkwood, 69), Rowbotham (for Broddle, 90)

27 November 1994
League Cup Final

Raith Rovers 2 Celtic 2 AET

(Raith Rovers won 6-5 on penalties)
Ibrox Stadium, Glasgow
Attendance: 45,384
Goals: Crawford (19), Dalziel (87); Walker (32), Nicholas (84)

Raith Rovers
  1 Thomson
  2 McAnespie
  3 Broddle
  4 Narey
  5 Dennis
  6 Sinclair
  7 Crawford
  8 Dalziel
  9 Graham
 10 Cameron
 11 Dair
Subs: Rowbotham (for Broddle, 93), Redford (for Dalziel, 112),
Potter (unused)

Celtic
  1 Marshall
  2 Galloway
  3 Boyd
  4 McNally
  5 Mowbray
  6 O'Neill
  7 Donnelly
  8 McStay
  9 Nicholas
 10 Walker
 11 Collins
Subs: Falconer (for Donnelly, 93), Byrne (for Nicholas, 98),
Bonner (unused)

Cup final statistics

Shots on – Raith 5 Celtic 7
Shots off – Raith 5 Celtic 16
Corners – Raith 5 Celtic 10
Throw-ins – Raith 37 Celtic 52
Free kicks – Raith 11 Celtic 14
Goal kicks – Raith 33 Celtic 7
Offsides – Raith 1 Celtic 1
Cautions – Raith 1 Celtic 1

13 May 1995
First Division

Hamilton 0 Raith Rovers 0
Firhill, Glasgow
Attendance: 5,333

 1 Thomson
 2 McAnespie
 3 Broddle
 4 Narey
 5 Dennis
 6 Raeside
 7 Nicholl
 8 Dalziel
 9 Dair
10 Cameron
11 Sinclair
Subs: Wilson (for Dair, 64), Kirkwood (unused), Allan (unused)

27 March 2011
Ronnie Coyle Benefit Match

Raith Rovers 1994 3 Celtic 1994 3
(Celtic 1994 won 4-2 on penalties)
Stark's Park, Kirkcaldy
Attendance: 2,729
Goals: Brewster, Lennon, Hetherston; Slaven, McMenamin 2

Raith Rovers 1994
Coach: Jimmy Nicholl

Team: Gordon Arthur, Scott Thomson, Paul Smith, John McGlynn, Craig Brewster, Shaun Dennis, Ally Graham, David Narey, Gary Pallister, Colin Harris, Stevie Crawford, David Sinclair, Jason Dair, Jason Rowbotham, Peter Hetherston, Gordon Dalziel, Paul Sweeney, George Wilson, Julian Broddle, Denis Irwin, Danny Lennon, Colin Cameron

Celtic 1994
Coach: Frank Connor

Team: Pat Bonner, Gordon Arthur, Mark McNally, Tom Boyd, Jackie McNamara, Willie McStay, Paul McStay, Raymond McStay, Joe Miller, Gerry Britton, Simon Donnelly, Andy Walker, Paul Elliot, Bernie Slaven, Paul Byrne, Colin McMenamin

BIBLIOGRAPHY

Most of the quotations contained in this book were obtained through direct interviews with the following individuals: Julian Broddle, Craig Brewster, Colin Cameron, Frank Connor, Stevie Crawford, Jason Dair, Gordon Dalziel, Tony Fimister, Richard Gordon, Ally Graham, Alex Kilgour, Stephen McAnespie, John McStay, Paul McStay, Jimmy Nicholl, Brian Potter, David Sinclair, Graeme Scott, Scott Thomson and John Valente.

Raith Rovers match programmes, 1986–1994

Fife Free Press, match reports and various articles, Graeme Scott and John Greechan, 1985–1994

Selected interviews from *Around with Greer* including Craig Brewster, Chris Candlish, Ronnie Coyle, Colin Harris, Andy Harrow, Martin Harvey, Peter Hetherston, Davie Kirkwood, Brian Potter, David Sinclair, Scott Thomson and Donald Urquhart, Stark's Bark Fanzine, John Greer, 1994–2003

Raith Rovers Football Supporters' Club 75th Anniversary Handbook, Jim Foy, 2001

Raith Rovers – That Was The Team That Was, BBC Scotland, 16 February, 2007

Interview with Jimmy Nicholl, *Scotsman*, 16 July 2010

The Football Years – Raith Rovers' League Cup Success, Chick Young, Scottish Television, 8 March 2011

Chapter 14: Dancing on the Streets of Raith, *Scottish Football. It's Not All About The Old Firm*, Scott Burns, Pitch Publishing 2012

Raindrops Keep Falling On My Head: My Autobiography, Ian Redford, Black and White Publishing, 2013

Tannadice Legends – Dave Narey, Dundee United official website, 2013

Interview with Jason Rowbotham, the official matchday magazine of Raith Rovers Football Club 2013/14, John Greer, 13 October 2013

Jimmy Can't Choose, Interview with Jimmy Nicholl, Ramsdens Cup Final official programme, Michael Grant, 6 April 2014

The following publications were valuable sources of statistics and background information.

Raith Rovers: A Promotion Diary, Raith Rovers Football Club, 1987

A History of Raith Rovers, John Litster, 1988

Raith Rovers Yearbook 1992/93, Raith Rovers Football Club, 1993

Always Next Season: 125 Years Of Raith Rovers Football Club 1883–2008, John Litster, Programme Monthly, 2008.

Raith Rovers Football Club 1991/92–1995/96, Tony Fimister, Tempus Publishing Limited, 2002

Rovers Greats, David Potter, The Raith Trust, 2008

Rovers Recalled, Raith Rovers In Pictures Through The Years – Volume 1, John Litster, Undated